THE ESSENTIAL CRAZY WISDOM

The Essential Crazy Wisdom

Wes "Scoop" Nisker

Ten Speed Press
Berkeley / Toronto

Ten Speed Press
PO Box 7123
Berkeley, California 94707
www.tenspeed.com

Distributed in Australia by Simon and Schuster Australia, in Canada by Ten Speed Press Canada, in New Zealand by Southern Publishers Group, in South Africa by Real Books, in Southeast Asia by Berkeley Books, and in the United Kingdom and Europe by Airlift Book Company.

Cover and interior design by Betsy Stromberg

Library of Congress Cataloging-in-Publication Data

Nisker, Wes.
    Essential crazy wisdom / Wes "Scoop" Nisker.
        p. cm.
    ISBN 1-58008-346-3
    1. Philosophy—History. 2. Wisdom—History. 3.
Paradox—History.   I. Title.
    B72 .N574 2001
    109—dc21
                                        2001003892
First printing, 2001
Printed in Canada

2 3 4 5 6 7 8 9 10 — 06 05 04 03 02

Contents

Acknowledgments

I gratefully acknowledge the many people who in so many ways contributed to the writing of this book. My deepest love and gratitude go to my daughter Rose who is such a joy in my life; to my wife and soul mate Terry Vandiver; and to Mudita, a dear companion on many paths.

I offer special thanks to all of my meditation teachers and to my close friends and spiritual mentors Joseph Goldstein and Jack Kornfield.

This book would be less than what it is without the excellent guidance of my friend and editor Shoshana Alexander. I also extend love and thanks to: Jan Buffum for keeping the family together; to Catherine Ingram, whose sympathetic ear were never more than a phone call away; to Perry Garfinkel for being a brother in so many ways and to Ariana Garfinkel for being Rose's friend; to Barbara Gates and the entire staff of *Inquiring Mind* for their encouragement; to Robert Fraser for scientific consultations about nothing and *for* nothing; to Djuna Odegard for her enthusiasms; to Jeff Greenwald for his irrepressible wit and tough-love critiques; and to Dan Clurman for keeping my computer humming through it all, with a little language philosophy thrown in for good measure.

I offer heartfelt appreciation to Phil Wood at Ten Speed Press for believing in me and letting me write the book I wanted to write. Also, I extend very special thanks to Mariah Bear and Carrie Rodrigues, whose editorial advice was extremely valuable throughout this endeavor. Also, thanks to Sal Glynn and the entire Ten Speed staff for their amiable assistance, and to George Young, whose sagacity guided the manuscript into book form.

Introduction

> Things are not as they seem. Nor are they otherwise.
>
> THE LANKAVATARA SUTRA

To begin, I would like to thank all of the people who found their way to the previous version of this book, making it a national bestseller by word-of-mouth. I actually haven't had to change much for this new edition, mostly because our species does not evolve fast enough to get too far ahead of the crazy wisdom we already have.

In these pages you will find Charlie Chaplin and Lily Tomlin shuffling around arm in arm with the stately and serene Gautama Buddha, with a few Taoists and Dadaists paradoxing along behind. Essentially, I am paying tribute to my teachers and heroes by introducing them to each other and letting them hang out together in this book, uniting them under the rubric of *crazy wisdom*.

I first encountered the phrase *crazy wisdom* in my study of Buddhism and Taoism, where it is sometimes used to describe the insights and teaching methods of the most radical masters of the Way. In my studies, I also discovered a profound similarity between the crazy wisdom of the Asian sages and that of certain Western philosophers, artists, and scientists, in particular the existentialists, the Dadaists, the Romantic and Beat poets, quantum physicists, and evolutionary biologists. As I continued to explore the similarities, a pattern began to emerge that eventually became the fabric of *The Essential Crazy Wisdom*.

I consider this book an excellent primer for survival in the new millennium we have entered. It offers the relatively timeless understanding and advise of clowns, jesters, tricksters, and holy fools, and hopefully they will be able to inspire a little more crazy wisdom in your own life. If I had to summarize their message—although many would deny that they even have one—it is that we are all stuck together in this moment of history, and the most appropriate response to each other is compassion and a sharing of laughter. After all, we really don't have a clue as to what is going on here, if anything, and most likely we aren't really in charge of very much of it anyway, and in the end the joke seems to be on all of us. Knowing that, we can relax a little and dispense with any blame. So far, as human beings, our greatest gifts, aside from the ability to make good painkillers, are our feelings of love and senses of humor. This book is a tribute to those qualities, as they have so generously appeared in members of our species to date.

    —Wes Nisker
       October 27, 2001
       Oakland, California

CHAPTER 1

In the Beginning...

> Where can I find a man who has forgotten words?
> I would like to have a word with him.
>
> CHUANG-TZU

To see the truth, contemplate all phenomena as a lie.

THAGANAPA

A special kind of wisdom is loose in the world. This wisdom is difficult to codify or categorize; and it refuses to be institutionalized. It is called *crazy* wisdom. And so it is, both crazy and wisdom.

Crazy wisdom is the wisdom of the saint, the Zen master, the poet, the mad scientist, and the fool. Crazy wisdom sees that we live in a world of many illusions, that the emperor has no clothes, and that much of human belief and behavior is ritualized nonsense. Crazy wisdom loves paradox and puns and pie fights and laughing at politicians.

You will find crazy wisdom flowing through all of human history, bubbling up here and there, now and then, pointing out different ways of looking at things, reminding people to take it easy, and providing a necessary counterpoint to self-righteousness. From the Taoists to the Dadaists; from the Book of Ecclesiastes to Mark Twain's *Letters to the Earth*, in the parables of Chuang-Tzu and the Baal Shem Tov, out of the cyclonic whirl of Rumi's dervish poetry and the profound nonsense of Samuel Beckett's confused characters, lurking beneath the unruly hair of Albert Einstein and between the bushy eyebrows of Groucho Marx, inside the howly voice of Allen Ginsberg and the crazed rantings of Lily Tomlin's bag lady: Whatever tone it speaks in and whatever disguise it wears, crazy wisdom arises again and again to expose us to ourselves and to remind us of the strange impossible nature of our enterprise here on earth—life.

Crazy wisdom is the skeptical voice inside us that doubts our importance in the world and questions our belief in a higher purpose. It is the nagging suspicion that both our reasons and our reasoning are mistaken.

Crazy wisdom laughs at our ridiculous ways and shows compassion for the suffering that results from them. It presents us with the bigger picture, and with ways to step lightly through it.

Crazy wisdom is the humbling knowledge of the immensity of the cosmos and the inevitable change and transformation that will ultimately wear away all our achievements. It is the grinning face of death, and the hollow sound of our question "Why?" echoing back at us from the void.

> If you understand, things are just as they are. If you
> do not understand, things are just as they are.
>
> ZEN BUDDHIST SAYING

Although we have no records to prove it, a little crazy
wisdom must have been around even in prehistoric times.
No doubt some contrary ancient sage was present to tell
the cave people that capturing fire would create as many
problems as it would solve. Crazy wisdom must be at
least as old as conventional wisdom. Every god has both
believers and disbelievers. True and false are constant
companions.

The Challenger

One essential principle of crazy wisdom can be found in its
name: It is crazy wisdom, not conventional wisdom. Many
people included in our crazy wisdom lineage would tell
you that crazy wisdom is the only wisdom, and that conventional wisdom is just the commonly agreed-upon lies of
any given era.

Conventional wisdom is the unexamined life, lost in
the mad rush of accumulation, lulled to sleep by the easy

lies of political hacks and newspaper scribblers, or by priests who wouldn't know a god if they met one. Crazy wisdom is the challenge to all that.

> Happy is it to practice the yoga of renouncing one's own country.
>
> MILAREPA, TIBETAN YOGI

What Do You Know, Anyway?

If crazy wisdom knows anything, it is that we don't know. We don't know who we are, where we are, or what this life and universe are about. We may be able to describe the world as we see it, give names to things, and even tentatively understand how some processes work, but we don't have a clue as to *why* things are the way they are. Or why they are at all.

> What's fire? You can tell me about oxidation, but that doesn't tell me a thing.
>
> JOSEPH CAMPBELL

We can explain how the respiratory system functions, but who can speak of the mystery of breath? Even if we think

I don't make jokes. I just watch the government and report the facts.

WILL ROGERS

The only thing that we can know is that we know nothing and that is the highest flight of human reason.

LEO TOLSTOY

Everything you know is wrong.

THE FIRESIGN THEATER

we understand the evolution of the human species, we still don't know where it's going next or why it developed in the first place. Although many spiritual schools claim to lead to self-knowledge, we cannot know ourselves completely. It is impossible to see the exact nature of a box when you are inside of it.

We may admit that we cannot know the *ultimate* meaning of life, yet we still assume that we can and will understand the laws of nature and how the universe works. However, looking back through history at our knowledge of the world, we find that basic "facts" change with every century and every civilization. By now it should be evident that what we know, or think we know, is perceived through a dense series of veils—culture, language, historical moment, and biological development. We and the world around us are always hidden from ourselves by ourselves.

How is it possible to find meaning in a finite world, given my waist and shirt size?

WOODY ALLEN

We Think Too Much

> Many complain of their looks, but none complain of
> their brains.
>
> YIDDISH PROVERB

Another claim of crazy wisdom is that humans don't know
how to think. Or maybe we just think too much. In either
case, what passes for reason often turns out to be unreason-
able in the end. Our so-called rational mind is deeply conditioned, biologically, psychologically, and culturally, and
what is labeled reasoning is often just the mind making
excuses for emotional needs and bad behavior. Reason has
become our ideology, but we may not yet be able to tell it
apart from wishful thinking. Perhaps the intellect is over-
valued and even overdeveloped. It may be that we think so
much we can't think, and know so much we don't know
anything.

> The evolution of the brain not only overshot the needs
> of prehistoric man, it is the only example of evolution
> providing a species with an organ which it does not
> know how to use.
>
> ARTHUR KOESTLER

A man's worst enemies can't
wish on him what he can
think up himself.

YIDDISH PROVERB

Reason may be humanity's greatest boon, but it is also our bitterest curse, perhaps even our fatal flaw. Reason gives us some degree of mastery over our world, and at the same time separates us from that world.

The act of thinking can be tiresome and is often painful. Sometimes it feels like we are locked into the prison of our mind and given a life sentence. Our punishment is to suffer under a life of sentences; the train of thought runs over our lives.

> Man's great misfortune is that he has no organ, no kind of eyelid or brake, to mask or block a thought, or all thoughts, when he wants to.
>
> PAUL-TOUSSAINT-JULES VALÉRY

Reason and the intellect are important tools for survival, as well as natural wonders that give us the capacity to create great flying machines and figures of speech. However, it appears that reason and the intellect only prepare the ground for crazy wisdom, which—like the universe itself—often seems to blossom out of nothingness. Even the greatest scientists say that it is not the rational mind that comes up with the most significant discoveries; something else is taking place.

We Think Too Much of Ourselves

> Man, here's your greatness: your meat is useless,
> your bones don't make ornaments, your skin can't
> be played on an instrument.
>
> KABIR

Crazy wisdom does not believe that humans, as individuals or as a species, are necessarily the ultimate purpose for the universe—the reason for the existence of billions of galaxies full of suns and planets and eons and eons of time. By force of habit, unyielding vanity, or perhaps a genetically encoded belief, we still think and behave as though the whole show was created for our sake and that our own history is somehow the major concern of the cosmos. Such a belief might be reasonable if we also still believed the sun goes around the earth. We should know better by now. As science pushes back the boundaries of space and time, it also calls our significance into question.

The most radical crazy wisdom does not view our personal human history (or even the evolution of the species) as movement toward a higher state. What makes us believe that things are advancing? Who is to say that we are better off now than we ever were? For that matter, who is to say that we are better off now than before we were at all?

> Belief in progress is a doctrine of idlers and Belgians.
> CHARLES-PIERRE BAUDELAIRE

Looking at the human species today, we can only guess that evolution is not yet finished. If we *are* the end product, then the cosmic design must be somewhat flawed. Furthermore, if we don't mutate soon into a smarter species of homo, we will probably go the way of the dinosaurs. In spite of our bumbling and often cruel ways, crazy wisdom has great love and compassion for humanity. If it doesn't always appear that way, it's just because some of the heavy melodrama and sentimentality have been removed from the story.

> For the present, the comedy of existence has not yet "become conscious" of itself. For the present, we still live in the age of tragedy, the age of moralities and religions.
> FRIEDRICH NIETZSCHE

A Different Way of Knowing

The knowledge beyond knowledge is my knowledge.

KABIR

Crazy wisdom is about another way of knowing. Some call it intuition or vision. Artists might say they are touched by the Muses, while some spiritual masters refer to direct seeing, revelation, or the wisdom that surpasses understanding. Some modern sages say crazy wisdom comes to us through a different part of the brain, perhaps the mysterious right hemisphere.

Whatever the pathway or process might be, in order to hear crazy wisdom we need to somehow shut off or turn down the grinding noise of the rational, analytic gears. Crazy wisdom requires that we get at least a little bit out of our minds. This can be done through prayer, meditation, nature, art, poetry, stories, and song.

Behead yourself!

RUMI

Some pathways to crazy wisdom are more direct than others. The spiritual masters, especially those in the Orient, have invented many techniques to move people out of their rational minds and into another mode of understanding. Unsolvable puzzles, repetitious chanting, elaborate visualizations, and even shouts, frights, and well-timed physical blows are used to drive people "crazy wise."

Another way people get wise and crazy is by gaining many perspectives: by changing points of view, getting into another place or a distant space and looking at things from there; by finding an odd angle, climbing high for an overview, seeing what is behind it all or underneath it all, stepping outside or going inside. With all due respect to Albert Einstein, crazy wisdom has known for a long time that a lot depends on where you're standing and how fast you're going.

> Sometimes I go about pitying myself,
> and all the time
> I am being carried on great winds across the sky.
>
> OJIBWAY SAYING

Nothing Is Real

> We now know that the moon is demonstrably not there when nobody looks.
>
> PHYSICIST N. DAVID MERMIN

> The inherent baselessness of physical and mental objects is called reality.
>
> AVATAMSAKA SUTRA

Crazy wisdom has always suspected that the world is not what it appears to be. The saints and sages have been trying to tell us this for ages through the languages of mysticism and poetry. Now contemporary scientists are saying much the same thing in terms of physics, biology, and astronomy. According to the scientists, "reality" is even stranger than anyone imagined.

The latest scientific theory proposes that the world may not even exist if someone is not here to perceive it. Modern science has literally pulled the rug out from under us. Quantum mechanics turned the physical world into a lying, deceiving scoundrel and made our own five senses and central nervous systems into co-conspirators in an elaborate "reality sting," a fraud carried on

Reality is a wave function traveling both backward and forward in time.

JOHN L. CASTRI

successfully since time immemorial. *We are constantly being deceived!*

Science is revealing worlds so enormous and so tiny and so strange that they must be the jokes of some creator who doubles over with laughter every time another bizarre twist to the reality puzzle is discovered. From superclusters of galaxies that measure hundreds of millions of light-years across to particles so small that they have no mass; from the Principle of Indeterminacy to a universe containing multiple realities, everything appears to be something other than what it appears to be. If scientists can be believed, the fact of the matter is that matter is not a fact. Nobody seems to have a clue as to what is going on.

Meanwhile, we have another "real" problem—ourselves. As Sigmund Freud wrote: "The unconscious is the true psychic reality; in its inner nature it is just as much unknown to us as the reality of the external world, and it is just as imperfectly communicated to us by the data of consciousness as is the external world by the reports of our sense-organs."

It is not only the external world that deceives us, but our internal world as well. For centuries mystics and poets have told us that we are not who we think we are, and that, in fact, we have no separate "self." Few have taken them seriously, thinking they were only being poetical and mystical. Now psychologists and biologists tell us something similar in terms of genes, chemicals, and early conditioning. The conclusion scientists are approaching but do not yet have the audacity to state is that we do not own our lives. The idea of a separate autonomous self is as much of an illusion as the world of matter.

> When you eventually see
> through the veils to how things really are,
> you will keep saying again
> and again,
> "This is certainly not like
> we thought it was!"
>
> RUMI

Do what you will, this
Life's a Fiction
And is made up of
Contradiction.

WILLIAM BLAKE

The Truths Will Set Us Free

What we are calling crazy wisdom is an enterprise of exposing the many sides of truth until there is no truth, and that's the truth. Crazy wisdom shows us the part of ourselves that Christians disapprovingly call our animal nature—the Coyote in us all—or the part of us that the Zen master might call our "original face." Crazy wisdom looks at things from the sky above and the mud below, through a telescope and a microscope, from the head and the heart and the loins, all in the hope that we will gain varied perspectives and play our roles in this bittersweet melodrama of life with a little more ease and grace. But wait! This doesn't mean crazy wisdom will necessarily solve our problems or save the planet.

> Everything is going to become unimaginably worse, and never get better again. If I lied to you about that, you would sense that I'd lied to you, and that would be another cause for gloom.
>
> KURT VONNEGUT, JR.

This process of revelation may, indeed, turn out to be somewhat uncomfortable. Crazy wisdom removes our masks and costumes, takes away our clocks, compasses, and house keys, and calls into question our most cherished beliefs in God, country, family, and future. All visions, including nightmares, must be addressed. Crazy wisdom even finds it important to remind us that we will die.

> We die, and we do not die.
>
> SHUNRYU SUZUKI

While some of crazy wisdom's revelations sound harsh, others are joyous and full of wonder. In fact, there may be an equal amount of each type, or at least two different ways of looking at everything. Crazy wisdom's insights inspire a wide range of responses, from pessimism and gloom to great ecstasy. But even in a critical mood, those who possess crazy wisdom will often soften up a hard-edged insight with a song, a poem, humor, or a little sleight of hand.

> Only the shallow know themselves.
> OSCAR WILDE

In this book we will weave the various threads of crazy wisdom together into a crazy quilt, perhaps an insecurity blanket—one that won't necessarily keep us warm at night but can make us more alive during the day. Through many cultures and characters, we will search for the common motifs to pattern our cloth, a patchwork we hope will hold together. At the very least, this crazy wisdom quilt may serve as a cover for some of our more wild ideas and unconventional impulses. Some people might even end up wearing it as a robe.

Since everything is but an apparition, perfect in being what it is, having nothing to do with good or bad, acceptance or rejection, one may well burst out in laughter.

LONG CHEN PA,
TIBETAN MEDITATION MASTER

We will meet many disparate characters who embody crazy wisdom. They will include sweet, gentle beings such as St. Francis of Assisi, who would go to great trouble to spare the life of a single earthworm. There will also be sharp-edged curmudgeons, the likes of Friedrich Nietzsche or H. L. Mencken, who would pull on the tail of all our sacred cows. Crazy wisdom is the fulcrum on which good and bad balance perfectly, the carousel on which both saint and sinner ride. As we meet these characters, it will be up to you, the reader, to decide—if you care to make any such distinctions—who is sinner and who is saint. After all, one person's Harpo Marx may be another's Meher Baba (both were silent). Deciding who sits on the higher throne, Jesus of Nazareth or Mark Twain, is up to each individual. Even the physicists have "proven" that reality depends on the observer. Revelation, like everything else, is in the eyes of the beholder.

In the process of exploring crazy wisdom, we may stumble across some truth. Even if we do, we might not recognize it. Or if we did, we would pick it up, and before you could say "quark" or "synapse," it would disappear right out of our hands. Just like this introduction to crazy wisdom will now vanish into the rest of this book.

CHAPTER 2

The Cast

> You may never get to touch the Master, but you can tickle his creatures.

THOMAS PYNCHON

Crazy wisdom makes its appearance through archetypal characters who arise in every culture to challenge convention. The clown, the jester, the trickster, and the fool are the four crazy wisdom archetypes. Although they have been known to trade costumes and steal each other's riffs and magic tricks, each challenges us in their own special way—with questions, stories, or laughter, or by offering their own radically different version of reality. Because these characters have devised some brilliant disguises it may appear that they have nothing at all to do with wisdom. Some of them put on masks in order to unmask us. Others remove all their masks. Some will mimic or mime to show us who we are.

The common message conveyed by the four archetypal characters is the crazy wisdom of doubt. Clowns and jesters have grave doubts about our attitude. "Is this seriousness really appropriate?" Others, such as the spiritual crazy wisdom masters—the holy fools—call into question our entire understanding of ourselves and the world.

The four archetypes share an uncanny ability to escape the trouble they inevitably get themselves into: The clown gets bopped, the trickster is dismembered and blown apart, the jester may have his head cut off by the king or be hit by rotten fruit thrown from the audience, and the great fool is about to fall off a cliff or be martyred by an angry mob. But just when it seems that all is lost, they rise again, recovered and whole, even from death. (The dismembered Coyote reassembles; Jesus Christ rises into everlasting life.) Because of their humor or their innocence, or because their revelations are so important, these crazy wisdom characters are immortal.

Although these four are at times banished from the institutions of church and state, they can often be found hanging out with the common folk. Over time, they have made their way into the stories, legends, and songs of the people.

The Clown

> The comic spirit masquerades in all things we say and
> do. We are each a clown and do not need to put on a
> white face.
>
> JAMES HILLMAN

The most human of the crazy wisdom archetypes is the
clown. The clown's too-big mouth is grotesquely grinning
or super sad, mocking our mortal moods. We laugh because
the clown is one of us, pathetic and lovable, trying hard,
but always flailing and failing. (Shy about being introduced,
the clown leans over to tie his shoe and . . . oh, no, the
inevitable tangled-up tango begins! Accompanied by silly
circus music.)

The clown shows us our awkward human condition
and encourages us to laugh at ourselves. We all are clowns,
always getting fouled up, mixed up, thwarted by circum-
stance. We climb the ladder only to find it is leaning against
the wrong wall. We search for hats that are already on our
heads. We plan our days only to find that the days have
other plans.

The clown points out our vulnerability. Although he is
eager and hopeful, we know he will not succeed. His great

triumph is the sheepish grin or silly shrug he displays after his failures. "Oh, well, that's the way it goes." The clown quickly forgets the past and moves on to the next disaster.

The clown's world, in which all of us live, is not a practical joke—it is an *impractical* joke. It is the world of Laurel and Hardy moving a piano, or of Elmer Fudd trying to get wid of the wabbit. In this world, appliances don't work right. We try to clean things up but in the process make them even dirtier. Just having a body sometimes seems an absurd condition. We run in circles wearing shoes that don't fit, getting nowhere and get blisters on the way. ("Aye, there's the rub.") The clown is living proof of the second law of thermodynamics: in this world, all things tend toward chaos and dissolution.

The clown is the everyman figure, personified by Charlie Chaplin caught in the machinery of modern times, or lured to the gold rush with the rest of the crowd. He is the unfortunate immigrant, the ordinary sadsack guy buffeted by the forces of history and his own foolishness, yet surviving somehow, sometimes managing a foolish grin, and occasionally even jumping up and clicking his worn-out heels as he walks into the sunset. The clown falls over for us, and stands up for us, too.

In the end, everything is a gag.
CHARLIE CHAPLIN

Some say the clown's white face is the mask of death, grinning at our feeble attempts to create order and meaning out of life's three-ring circus. In the end, says the white face, we are always the butt of the joke.

The clown is the lighter side of dark forces, chaos made benign, the subconscious as silly. The clown is the most acceptable and lovable of all the crazy wisdom archetypes.

> The clown is the primitive comedian.
> GEORGE SANTAYANA

The Jester

> No matter how much restriction civilization imposes on the individual, he nevertheless finds some way to circumvent it. Wit is the best safety valve modern man has evolved; the more civilization, the more repression, the more need there is for wit.
>
> SIGMUND FREUD

Jesters are the wits and critics. They expose the establishment's lies and make light of the contemporary social scene. While the clown reveals the timeless foibles of humanity, the jester takes on the social and political behavior specific to the current age.

The jester has appeared in many guises: as playwright and pamphleteer, roaming minstrel and balladeer, actor in the commedia dell'arte, master of ceremonies at a caberet or vaudeville show; as cartoonist, satirist, parody writer; and as the contemporary stand-up comedian.

> No matter how cynical you get, it is impossible to keep up.
> LILY TOMLIN

Unlike the all-too-human clown, sometimes the jester is barely human—a character whose teeth and tongue are equally sharp. ("Doesn't that slay you.") He gets away with dangerous revelations by making them funny.

The jester works with words. While the clown mimes, the jester may mimic. As has been said, the pen is mightier than the sword. The jester slices the *s* off *sword* and thrusts with the word. The jester jousts with his sharp tongue, hurling barbs, needles, jabs, sticking it to them, laying them low, killing them.

> Seriousness is the only refuge of the shallow.
> OSCAR WILDE

The jester takes the wind out of politicians' sails, deflates inflated rhetoric, punctures hypocrisy and hypeocracy, bureaucracy and bore-ocracy, until they are shown to be nothing but hot air, the laughable breeze made by humans fawning over themselves and flapping their jaws.

The court jester is the king's own fool and often his best advisor. While others are afraid to tell the king the truth, the court jester, playing the fool, points out both the king's weaknesses and the political realities. He had better be funny because his head is at stake.

The aim of a joke is not to degrade the human being but to remind him that he is already degraded.

GEORGE ORWELL

> FOOL: The sweet and bitter fool
> Will presently appear;
> The one in motley here,
> The other found out there.
> LEAR: Dost thou call me fool, boy?
> FOOL: All thy other titles thou hast given away:
> That thou wast born with.

WILLIAM SHAKESPEARE
The Tragedy of King Lear

One of the jester's most famous tracts came from the pen of Jonathan Swift during the Irish famine in the early 1700s. In the following excerpt from "A Modest Proposal," Swift's *biting* sarcasm lays bare society's indifference to the suffering of the poor.

> I have been assured by a very knowing American of my acquaintance in London, that a young healthy child

well nursed is at a year old most delicious, nourishing
and wholesome food, whether stewed, roasted, baked
or boiled, and I make no doubt that it will equally
serve in a fricassee, or a ragout.

I do therefore humbly offer it to public consideration,
that of the hundred and twenty thousand children
already computed, twenty thousand may be reserved
for breed, whereof only one fourth part to be males,
which is more than we allow to sheep, black-cattle,
or swine. . . . That the remaining hundred thousand may
at a year old be offered in sale to the persons of quality
and fortune, through the kingdom, always advising the
mother to let them suck plentifully in the last month, so
as to render them plump, and fat for a good table.

The jester also challenges religious beliefs, perhaps never
more thoroughly than in the artistry of Mark Twain. His
most irreverent writing, collected in *Letters from Earth,*
was not published until the 1940s, nearly thirty years after
Twain's death. If sections of this book had been released in
his lifetime, Twain might well have been lynched. In it he
dares to take on none other than Jehovah Himself.

He says, naively, outspokenly, and without suggestion
of embarrassment: "I the Lord thy God am a jealous
God." You see, it is only another way of saying, "I the
Lord thy God am a small God; a small God, and fretful

about small things." He was giving a warning: he could not bear the thought of any other God getting some of the Sunday compliments of this comical little human race. . . .

The jester works with words, sometimes making words themselves the target. The joker or punster creates confusion and laughter by showing us that words often have two meanings—the double entendre or the Freudian slip. Sometimes the truth is in the mistake, and in the misspoken word we hear the true meaning behind the intended meaning. At other times there is no meaning there at all.

> One morning I shot an elephant in my pajamas. How he got in my pajamas I don't know. Then we tried to remove the tusks, but they were embedded so firmly we couldn't budge them. Of course, in Alabama the Tuskaloosa. We took some pictures of the native girls, but they were not developed. But we're going back again.
>
> GROUCHO MARX

Nonsense either reveals the inherent meaninglessness of words or creates new meanings for them. The pun can be the lowest form of humor or the highest. In other words, some types of nonsense make more sense than others.

Hearasay in paradox lust.

JAMES JOYCE
Finnegans Wake

In *Finnegans Wake,* James Joyce created his own language, based on English but thickened with multilingual puns, onomatopoeia, and word associations that present the reader with a maze of meanings. With his sustained word-play and rhythms, Joyce makes the description of a sexual encounter resonate beyond ordinary language.

> Pharoah with fairy, two lie, let them! Yet they went it back qual his leif, himmertality, bullseaboob and rivishy divil, light in hand, helm on high, to peekaboo durk the thicket of slumbwhere, till their hour with their scene be struck for ever and the book of the dates he close, he clasp and she and she seegn her tour d'adieu, Pervinca calling, Soloscar hears (O Sheem! O Shaam!) and gentle Isad Ysut gag, flispering in the nightleaves flattery, dinsiduously, to Finnegan, to sin again and to make grim grandma grunt and grin again while the first grey streaks steal silvering by for to mock their quarrels in dollymount tumbling.

The greatest of word jesters can deconstruct a language and speak in strange tongues that we all understand. Words are only commonly agreed-upon sounds, when spoken, or symbols, when written. When the game is revealed as the game that it is, we are exposed, grunting and humming to one another in the elaborate music of language.

Instead of relying on words alone, some jesters venture into the streets or go to the seat of power to make their point, displaying crazy wisdom through their idiosyncratic behavior or through defiant acts of political theater.

Diogenes the Cynic, an infamous figure in ancient Greece, walked the streets of Athens with a lantern at night, telling people he was looking for an honest man. Diogenes, who despised worldly possessions and lived for a while in a bathtub, still gained much respect as a philosopher. When visiting Diogenes, Alexander the Great asked if he could do him a favor. Diogenes replied, "Yes. Remove your shadow." Legend has it that Diogenes once masturbated on the Parthenon steps, inviting those who masturbated in the privacy of their homes to join him in a public display.

The twentieth century demanded outrageous acts of defiance from its jesters, and they answered the call. In the late 1960s, the American counterculture staged many acts of protest through guerilla theater events. Yippies (members of the Youth International Party) threw money from the balcony of the New York Stock Exchange onto the trading floor below. To protest the Vietnam War, thousands of people surrounded the Pentagon and chanted "om" in unison in an attempt to levitate the massive building. According to unreliable sources, they did succeed.

Because jesters are naysayers, they often speak the truth by saying no to obvious lies, absurdities, and injustices. In the worldly realm of relative truths, jesters are the champions of crazy wisdom.

All "isms" should be "wasms."

ABBIE HOFFMAN

The Trickster

Since everybody laughs at me, I will laugh at them.

IKTOMI, OGLALA TRICKSTER

The tricksters are the rascals of myth and folklore. Sometimes they appear as bumbling creators of the world, the source of all our troubles; at other times they are nothing more than ribald sex fiends. Whichever role they play, the tricksters do not abide by ordinary codes of behavior. They emerge from a time before good and evil, and their crazy wisdom is to act out our uncivilized, primal nature. In *The Trickster,* Paul Radin explores the trickster's universality.

No generation understands him fully, but no generation can do without him. Each had to include him in all its theologies, in all its cosmologies, despite the fact that it realized that he did not fit properly into any of them, for he represents not only the undifferentiated and distant past, but likewise the undifferentiated present within each individual.

The mythical tricksters are a combination of god and beast, and are among the oldest human images of the divine. Although many people now believe in a more noble creator, some still think that the trickster is to blame for the way things are.

Radin recounts a Blackfoot Indian myth that tells how, when Old Man (the trickster) was creating things, he would have made a worse mess if it hadn't been for Old Woman. She insisted on helping Old Man decide how people should be fashioned. He agreed to listen only if *he* could have the final say; luckily it didn't work out that way.

"Well," said Old Man, "let the people have eyes and mouths in their faces; but they shall be straight up and down."

"No," said Old Woman. "We will not have them that way. We will have the eyes and mouths in the faces, as you say, but they shall all be set crosswise."

"Well," said Old Man, "the people shall have ten fingers on each hand."

"Oh no!" said Old Woman, "that will be too many. They will be in the way. There shall be four fingers and one thumb on each hand."

"Well," said Old Man, "we shall beget children. The genitals shall be at our navels."

"No," said Old Woman, "that will make child-bearing too easy and the people will not care for their children. The genitals shall be at the pubes."

When Coyote is given the role of creator, he always makes a mess of things. In the beginning, it is told, Coyote had a sack full of stars that he was supposed to place in the sky in neat rows. He was doing a good job at first, but then he got bored and finally tossed the remaining stars into the sky where they are now scattered randomly. How might the sky have looked if Coyote had taken more care?

The trickster also represents wild, unruly nature, arriving in the village to sniff around for some action. When Coyote visits the Indian tribes of North and Central America, he has absolutely no manners. It is even said that he laughs through his anus. By most accounts, he is also a shameless sex fiend, whom the Hopi call a "cunt-craving coyote," and in one story he even has sex with his own grandmother.

You might try to locate Coyote sometime. He seems to have survived the modern world better than some other tricksters, and he can still be seen around campfires and powwows, sneaking into *zendos,* or hanging around coffeehouses and red-light districts. In *Coyote's Journal,* a group of contemporary writers tell of coyote's ways.

Why Dogs Smell Each Other's Butts
BY LOWELL JAEGER

When he asked, the dogs refused him.
You are unclean, they told Coyote,
you are not a dog.
So the dogs undressed for their sweatbath
and entered the sweatlodge without him.

Coyote envied the glossy fur coats
the dogs had hung outside the lodge.
He thought of stealing them,
but decided not to.

Instead he threw the long coats
in a great pile,
and wiped his muddy feet across them.
Then he set fire to the sweatlodge roof
and said in a loud voice:
Oh what will the dogs do now,
Coyote has taken their fur!

From behind a rock, Coyote sat laughing
as the naked dogs rushed
into the cold out-of-doors,
grabbing for a coat,
afraid there might be too few
to cover everyone.

Years later, as the story goes,
with every dog zipped in someone else's fur,
dogs smell each other's butts,
looking for their own.

Meanwhile Coyote is still grinning,
off in the hills somewhere,
rolling in red dirt,
thinking how crude
to be a dog,

how much more clean,
how much more fun
to be Coyote.

Coyote is most often seen with his head back, muzzle facing
upward, howling at the moon. The secret of his crazy
wisdom can be understood by listening closely to his cry.
In it one can hear a bittersweet mixture of all experience;
both longing and laughter, mocking and moaning.

Even though he loves to steal the stage, Coyote is just one of the animal forms that the trickster takes. In North and Central American Indian tribes, he also appears as Raven, Crow, or Hare; in Europe as Reynard the Fox; in Africa as the spider Ananse; and in the American South as B'rer Rabbit.

Aspects of the trickster appear in the deities and mythical characters of many cultures. The Hindu's Lord Krishna is part trickster and loves to play jokes on mortals (if you were a god, wouldn't you?), especially the young girls, the milkmaids, whom he dazzles with his divine radiance and magic powers.

A West African trickster god named Edshu also loves to create uncertainty and chaos among humans. Once Edshu went for a walk, wearing a hat that was red on one side and white on the other. He walked down the path between two farmers' fields, waving at both of them and making sure they each saw his hat. Later, when the farmers talked to each other, they got into an argument over the hat's color, one having seen the red side and the other the white side. Just as they were ready to kill each other over this disagreement, Edshu revealed himself and his hat trick.

The fact that Coyote and other tricksters are making a comeback is evidence that the crazy wisdom of these mythological rascals refuses to be paved over. Where the brush begins to thicken, just outside the boundaries of our civilized encampment, the trickster howls at night to remind us of the chaos that lives all around.

The Fool

Lord, what fools these mortals be.

WILLIAM SHAKESPEARE

If the fool would persist in his folly,
he would become wise.

WILLIAM BLAKE

The fool is the most potent of the archetypes and also the most capable teacher of crazy wisdom. There are actually two types of fool: the foolish fool and the great fool. The foolish fool is inept and silly, a clown of the mind. The great fool is wise beyond ordinary understanding. The foolish fool is the one we see every day when we look into the mirror or walk down the street. The great fool is the rarest of beings.

Start a huge, foolish project, like Noah. It makes absolutely no difference what people think of you.

RUMI

Innocence is the trademark of both fools. The innocence of the foolish fool makes him clumsy and unsophisticated because he tries to live according to convention. The great fool, however, does not try to fit in; in his innocence, he lives by his own rules. The foolish fool and his money are soon parted, but the great fool gives his money away. The foolish fool always gets lost, while the great fool is at home everywhere. The great fool has different values from the rest of us and therefore is crazy wisdom's master of ceremonies.

> Einstein was a man who could ask immensely simple questions.
>
> JACOB BRONOWSKI
> *The Ascent of Man*

The great fool, like Einstein, wonders about the obvious and stands in awe of the ordinary, which makes him capable of revolutionary discoveries about space and time. The great fool lives outside the blinding circle of routine, remaining open to the surprise of each moment. We are the foolish ones, complacent in our understanding. We take for granted the miraculous dance of creation, but the great fool continuously sees it as if for the first time. The revelations of the great fool often show us where we are going, or—more often—where we are.

If others had not been foolish, we should be so.

WILLIAM BLAKE

The Fool Is a Card

The great fool is the first card in the tarot deck. He is the master of ceremonies, smiling and welcoming us to the show, the Grand Illusion, the parade of archetypal characters to follow. The Fool announces that what we are about to see is only a melodrama, and we should not take these masks or matters too seriously. Our personalities are just put-ons, personae, roles we are given to play. We read the lines and flesh out the scenes but there's really not much we can do about the plot. Our destiny, is, after all, written in the cards.

In the tarot the Fool is portrayed wandering in the sunshine with his knapsack and a little dog, seemingly without a care in the world and with no particular place to go. And he is about to step off the edge of a cliff! Perhaps the Fool knows he will go over the cliff but continues to smile because he also knows he will never hit bottom. Maybe the Fool understands that he, the cliff, and the bottom are all illusions.

The Fool is the only unnumbered card in the tarot deck; he is outside the boundaries of number or sequence, outside all categories, beyond good and evil. With the

Fool, anything can happen, and all things, even death, are equally worthy of his perpetual smile.

As a testament to his power, the Fool is one of the few characters from the tarot deck to make it into our modern playing cards. He becomes the joker—always wild, and almost always welcome. Like the Fool, the joker is without number or trump, and therefore above all numbers and trumps. He has no specific value and so is of the greatest value. The joker is mightier than the kings and higher than the aces.

Fool Around

The fool can be found playing the central role in folk stories around the world, acting out the part of either village idiot or eccentric sage. In the following story, Mulla Nasrudin, a notorious character throughout the Islamic world, is playing the great fool, teaching crazy wisdom to the people.

When Nasrudin was asked to speak to the congregation at the mosque, he went up to the front and asked, "Oh, people, do you know what I have come to tell you?" The crowd answered, "No." Nasrudin then said, "If you don't know what I have come to tell you, then you are too ignorant to understand what I was going to say." And he left the mosque. But the people knew he had great wisdom, so they invited him back the next week. This time when Nasrudin asked the congregation whether they knew what he was going to tell them, the crowd answered, "Yes." "Fine," said Nasrudin, "then I don't need to waste your time." And once again he left the mosque. But once again the people invited him back, thinking the next time they could convince him to talk. When he arrived the following week, Nasrudin again asked the congregation if they knew what he was going to tell them. This time, half of the people answered back "Yes," and half of them answered back "No." "Fine," said Nasrudin, "Then those who know should tell those who don't know, and I will be on my way."

There is a Chinese story about a wise farmer who knew about the impossibility of knowing and about the arbitrary nature of human judgments. In the story, the farmer's horse runs away, and his neighbor comes to offer sympathy, saying, "Too bad about your horse." The farmer simply replies, "Maybe." The next day the farmer's horse comes back leading two wild horses into the stable. This time the neighbor congratulates the farmer, saying, "What a lucky break!" Again the farmer replies, "Maybe." The next day the farmer's son breaks his leg trying to tame one of the wild horses, and again the neighbor comes over to offer sympathy. "Too bad," says the neighbor. Once again the farmer simply replies, "Maybe." The next day the recruitment officer from the king's army comes through the region taking all the young men of fighting age, but since the farmer's son has a broken leg he is left behind. The story can go on and on.

In each of these stories, a wise fool teaches us the impossibility of knowing anything for certain. Sometimes, however, the foolish fools get to be the teachers of crazy wisdom.

One day Nasrudin (who can play any kind of fool) was sitting in the marketplace in front of a basket full of hot peppers, eating one after the other. His eyes were watering, his face was red and contorted, and still he continued to eat the hot peppers. When someone finally asked him why he was doing this, Nasrudin replied, "I'm looking for a sweet one."

There is a Christian story of unknown origin, which concerns a foolish fool who is very religious. The most modern version of the story tells of this pious man living in a small town in Europe when a big flood occurs. As the water rises in the town and begins to fill the houses, a rescue boat comes to take the pious man to safety. However, the man waves the boat away, saying, "Don't worry about me. I believe in God, and He will save me." Later, as the water rises higher, the man is forced to climb up onto the roof of his house, and once again the boat comes by. Once again the pious man waves the boat away, crying, "Don't worry, I believe in God, and He will save me!" Finally, just as the waters reach the chimney and the man has to stand on tip-toe to breathe, a helicopter flies over and throws a rope down to him. However, the pious man refuses to grab the rope, and a few minutes later is swept away and drowns. When the pious man reaches heaven he gets an audience with God, and after bowing, he says with consternation, "My Lord, I was your faithful servant, who worshiped you daily, loving you and trusting in you, but when the flood came, you would not save me. Why, Lord, why?" God looks at the man with a puzzled expression and says, "That's odd. I was sure that I had sent you two boats and a helicopter."

In these folk stories we learn about the ways of fools and their extremes of wisdom and folly. However, it is vital to our saga of crazy wisdom that we meet some of the great fools in a historical context as well—in the flesh, so to speak. We will be surprised to discover that many of us pray to some form of the great fool daily. Our worship is directed toward those fools who became figureheads of the world's great religions.

The Holy Fools

> None attains to the Degree of Truth until a thousand honest people have testified that he is a heretic.
>
> JUNAID OF BAGHDAD, SUFI

The holy fools arise from spiritual subcultures, the esoteric and mystical underground of the world's great religious traditions. They know a different reality than the rest of us and live every moment in accordance with their understanding, no matter what the cost. They are divine madmen. Among the better known are Lao-tzu, Buddha, and Christ— all challengers of conventional truth; all masters.

Although today it may seem inappropriate to label these holy men "fools," they probably were called that in their own time. Certainly more people thought them foolish than wise.

Lao-tzu was a crazy visionary poet who reputedly turned down good jobs with the king in order to live secluded in the mountains. In the important circles of court and city life, they probably laughed when Lao-tzu's name was mentioned.

Gautama, the Buddha, was no doubt viewed as just one of the more popular cult leaders of his time. He set up communal dwellings in the forest, where he taught his followers to reject ordinary worldly pursuits and to replace them with an odd-sounding doctrine called "the middle path." If the Buddha were alive and teaching today, many parents would certainly arrange to have their children kidnapped from his community and deprogrammed.

In his own time, Jesus was considered a kook. He became a hero among the poor because he ministered to them, but respectable people probably saw him as a scruffy, wandering street person. Not only was Jesus labeled a fool, he sometimes accepted the role and deliberately played the fool as part of his radical protests.

> Some think, perhaps, that it is peace which I have come to cast upon the world. They do not know that it is dissension which I have come to cast upon the world.
>
> JESUS OF NAZARETH

> Like the jester, Christ defies custom and scorns crowned heads. Like a wandering troubadour, he has no place to lay his head. Like the clown in the circus parade, he satirizes existing authority by riding into town replete with regal pageantry when he has no earthly power.
>
> HARVEY COX
> *The Feast of Fools*

Many Eastern sages called themselves fools, and their acceptance of that label is a key to their crazy wisdom. Chuang-tzu said that anyone who knows he is a fool "is not the biggest fool."

The holy fools are found in two distinct streams of crazy wisdom. In one are the Taoists and Zen masters who learn to ride the currents and surrender to the flow. They become friends with insecurity, making doubt their guide and each moment their god. In the other stream, visionaries like Christ or the Sufi poet Rumi pass through doubt into the certainty of their own uncommon visions and lose themselves in the love of God or the oceanic Oneness,
living thereafter in an altered state.

> An image crosses the heart: "Return to your origin." The heart flutters all around and away from the world of colours and perfumes, clamoring: "Wherefore the Origin?" while tearing apart its adornments, because of its love.
>
> RUMI

Holy fools see through the veils of illusion to the unity of all existence. When Jesus proclaims he is the son of God, he is saying that we are all children of God, all emanating

A rabbi whose congregation does not want to drive him out of town isn't a rabbi.

HASIDIC SAYING

from the same divine source. So too, the Taoist or Zen master understands that all things are one, and our separate selves are just a painful illusion. To the most radical sages, even the simple act of naming is a habit that falsely separates us from the rest of creation.

Holy fools agree that false identification with the self fosters fear, hatred, and greed, which in turn result in violence and war. Consequently, holy fools usually live simply or in voluntary poverty. They believe that wealth builds up a false self and that too many possessions obscure the great view.

Identification with the poor almost inevitably forces the holy fools into the role of rebel, leading populist movements that shake up the existing political and religious orders. State and church tend to scratch each other's backs, and when you challenge one you threaten the other. The greatest of holy fools have been out of favor with the priesthood and often in trouble with the law.

Gautama, the Buddha, broke away from Hinduism to demonstrate that truth was not the exclusive realm of Brahman priests, and that salvation had nothing to do with caste, rituals, or offerings. The Buddha taught that anyone could practice liberation and achieve it.

> The Great Way is not difficult for those who have no preferences.
>
> THIRD ZEN PATRIARCH

It is easier for a camel to go through the eye of a needle, than for a rich man to enter into the kingdom of God.

JESUS OF NAZARETH

I do not call a man a Brahman because of his birth or of his mother. He is supercilious in his mode of address and he is wealthy: but the poor man who is free from attachments, him I call indeed a Brahman.

BUDDHA
The Dhammapada

Lao-tzu and the Taoists yanked on Confucius's beard and said, "The Way is the other way." The Taoists rejected the followers of Confucius and their stuffy moralism; their formal codes of duty to family and society. The Taoists understood that virtue does not come from obeying rules but from an inner understanding. They refused to be false to themselves and to the Tao, the nature of things.

Confucius will deck things out in feathers and paint, and conduct his affairs with flowery phrases, mistaking side issues for the crux. He is willing to distort his inborn nature in order to make himself a model for the people, not even realizing that he is acting in bad faith.

CHUANG-TZU

Jesus, a Jew, denounced for their corruption and collaboration with the Romans the Jewish establishment of Judea. He chased the money changers out of the synagogue, gave up all his possessions, and preached to the lowest classes. There is little doubt why the authorities called him mad and put him to death.

> For as the lightning flashes and lights up the sky from one side to the other, so will the Son of man be in his day. But first he must suffer many things and be rejected by this generation.
>
> LUKE 17:24

The Chan and Zen Buddhists overturned the priestly piety of the earliest Indian Buddhist schools. Influenced by the Chinese Taoists, many Zen masters rebelled against formalized teaching methods and adherence to scripture, creating their own practices and interpretations of the path as they went along. While the Indian Buddhists taught rejection of the world for the sake of enlightenment, most Zen masters refused to make any distinction between this world and another. Zen attempted to break down all dualities.

> No suffering, no origination, no stopping, no path, no cognition, also no attainment.
>
> HEART SUTRA, ZEN MAHAYANA TRADITION

> I would believe only in a god who could dance.
>
> FRIEDRICH NIETZSCHE

> In singing and dancing is the voice of the Law.
>
> HAKUIN ZEN MASTER

Whirling out of Islam came the Sufi masters, mad with dancing and chanting the names of God. They offered the faithful a simple means of knowing and loving Allah. Similarly, the Hasidic rabbis arose out of Judaism in the diaspora. In the midst of constant danger and uncertainty, they led the people in song and dance in praise of the Lord. The Baal Shem Tov declared that the peasant who sat at the back of the synagogue and could only whistle the prayers was as delightful to God as the learned scholar who could recite the Talmud. A similar message comes from the black Southern Baptist gospel tradition and the hypnotic, ecstatic singing of Krishna devotees: "If I can't dance, I don't want to be in your religion."

Holy fools are often religious revolutionaries. Some even write their own scriptures, or their lives become scripture. After their deaths come the charlatans, and then the churches. Chances are, if the great crazy wisdom masters who gave their names to the world's major religions came back today, they would, without exception, refuse to join their own churches.

A Fool for Now

Mohandas Gandhi, a great fool, was recently among us. With only a spinning wheel and a copy of the Hindu "Song of God," Gandhi, the *mahatma* or "great soul," challenged the British Empire and the whole of Western civilization. According to Gandhi, religion and politics are inseparable, and both should be lived according to the primary principle of nonviolence.

> When the practice of nonviolence becomes universal,
> God will reign on earth as He does in heaven.

Gandhi's nonviolence means refusing to harm or kill any living being, and is a complete way of life. This principle led Gandhi to employ tactics of nonviolent resistance against the British in India, and also formed the cornerstone for his ideal of village socialism.

> Centralization as a system is inconsistent with a
> nonviolent structure of society. By the nonviolent
> method, we seek not to destroy the capitalist,
> we seek to destroy capitalism.

Gandhi understood there would be violence as long as there were extremes of rich and poor in the world. When he was in Europe he saw how Western capitalism and urban life fostered greed and disharmony. Therefore, while most of the developing world rushed toward Western-style industrialization, Gandhi urged India to develop small cottage industries and foster cooperative village life. He believed that village society could save India from the evils of the twentieth century, and would set an example for the rest of the world to follow. In Gandhi's vision, only by living simply in small-scale communities could people find social harmony, individual happiness, or spiritual fulfillment.

> There is no limit to the measure of sacrifice that one may make in order to realize *oneness with all life,* but certainly that ideal will set a limit to your wants. That is the antithesis of the position of modern civilization which says, "Increase your wants."

Once, Gandhi visited England's King George wearing only a loincloth, shawl, and sandals. Later, when questioned about the propriety of his attire, Gandhi replied, "The King was wearing enough for both of us." On another occasion,

when Gandhi was asked what he thought of Western civilization, he answered, "I think it would be a good idea."

Like so many holy fools before him, Gandhi dedicated
his life to helping the poor, and he lived as one of them.
When he died, his only possessions were his spinning wheel,
a figurine of the See No Evil, Hear No Evil, Speak No Evil
monkeys, his spectacles and walking staff, and a few pieces
of homespun clothing.

The holy fools have had varying degrees of success
with their truths. Some of them found the right symbols and
metaphors for their time and—creating new myths out of
their own lives—were posthumously accorded the status
of deity. They gave humanity a miraculous rebirth, a new
beginning to the eternal cycle. Through their rebellious
visions and deeds these holy fools became founders of
new spiritual orders, new symbolic representations of the
meaning of it all.

> God has no religion.
> MAHATMA GANDHI

CHAPTER 3

Crazy Eastern Wisdom

The most complete expressions of a crazy wisdom point of view are contained in Taoism and Zen Buddhism. Neither is exactly a philosophy or a religion: the early masters of Taoism and Zen Buddhism did not promote a god or even much of a metaphysical system. They saw their state of grace as one of just "being"—living without ideology, analysis, or a higher meaning.

In their meditations, Eastern sages reached an understanding that would not develop in the West until nearly two thousand years later: They recognized that the human mind is thoroughly conditioned, and that the idea of a free agent "self" is an illusion. Furthermore, long before the Western world got a glimpse of just how big the universe is, Eastern sages seem to have intuitively grasped the enormity of space and time.

The crazy wisdom of Taoists and Zen masters may sound especially crazy to Westerners, and often not so wise. It does not justify existence. You don't pray to anything or even *do* much of anything. Sometimes you hardly move. Both truth and salvation are considered a matter of acceptance, of just being.

This very earth is the Lotus Land of purity,
And this very body is the Body of Buddha.
ZEN MASTER HAKUIN

Therefore the sage keeps to the deed that consists in taking no action and practices the teaching that uses no words.

LAO-TZU

How Now, Great Tao?

Lao-tzu and Chuang-tzu are the quintessential crazy wisdom masters and the founding fathers of Taoism, most easily described as a radical existential philosophy that emerged in China in the sixth to fifth centuries B.C. Lao-tzu is the reputed author of the Tao Te Ching, the fundamental Taoist text. He is the more serious of the two; the philosopher of paradox and vast perspective. Chuang-tzu is more of a storyteller, using parable and humor to mock ordinary understanding. Chuang-tzu asks:

> Who can look on non-being as his head, on life as his back, and on death as his rump? Who knows that life and death, existence and annihilation, are all a single body? I will be his friend.

Taoism's basic principle is that all things are one. Many spiritual traditions discuss fundamental unity, but Master Lao and Master Chuang draw the most extreme conclusions from this concept. For them, the unity of all things means that no distinction can be made between life and death, right and wrong, holy and profane, or any other "this and that." All are part of a single, evolving creation—the Tao. Master Tung-kuo once asked Chuang-tzu, "This thing called the Tao—where does it exist?" Chuang-tzu answered, "It is in the piss and dung." The unity of the Tao encompasses the piss and dung and the Taoists themselves.

Master Chuang and Master Lao understood that most of our problems are caused when we create a separate identity and special importance for ourselves. If we set ourselves apart from the rest of creation, we will inevitably come into conflict with it. The illusion that we are separate is the root of our suffering.

> Hope and fear are both phantoms
> that arise from thinking of the self.
> When we don't see the self as self,
> what do we have to fear?
>
> LAO-TZU

Lao-tzu knew that his crazy wisdom sounded like nonsense to most people. After all, he recommended that we give up our reasonable approach to life and our desire to understand, give up any idea we might have of *purposeful* existence, give up our pursuit of wealth or fame or happiness. He and Chuang-tzu suggested that we are going about this business of living the wrong way. Chuang-tzu has a suggestion:

> I cannot tell if what the world considers "happiness" is happiness or not. All I know is that when I consider the way they go about attaining it, I see them carried away headlong, grim and obsessed, in the general onrush of the human herd, unable to stop themselves or to change their direction. All the while they claim to be just on the point of attaining happiness. My opinion is that you never find happiness until you stop looking for it.

Zen What?

Shut your mouth, close your lips, and say something!
PAICHANG ZEN MASTER

In Zen, crazy wisdom reaches the limits of both craziness and wisdom. A great Zen sage cuts off his eyelids so he can meditate longer without falling asleep; a student cuts off his arm to demonstrate to the master that he is desperate for the teachings; one master shouts so loudly that his disciple, although "enlightened" by the shout, is also made deaf; and stories abound of masters and disciples hitting each other with their staffs.

Kwatz! (Ho!)
LIN-CHI, ZEN MASTER

When you say "yes," you get thirty blows of my staff; when you say "no," you get thirty blows of my staff just the same.

TOKUSAN

When you have a staff, I will give you one; when you have none, I will take it away from you.

HUI-CHI'ING

Kwan! (Ho!)
UMMON, ZEN MASTER

Zen, the hybrid of Taoism and Buddhism, sprouted in China in 600 A.D., and later spread to Japan, where it came into full bloom. However, many Zen followers trace their lineage back to India, 500 B.C., when the Buddha presented his teachings to a group of more than one thousand disciples at the Mount of the Holy Vulture. When it was time to speak, the Buddha paused, then simply held up a flower. Only one person in the entire assemblage, a monk named Kasyapa understood exactly what the Buddha meant, and he was immediately enlightened. According to some, Kasyapa's sudden, direct insight into the perfection of things as they are was the beginning of the path of Zen. This path is summed up by what are known as the Four Great Statements of Zen:

> A direct transmission outside the scriptures;
> No dependence on words and letters;
> Direct pointing to reality;
> Seeing into one's own nature and attaining
>   Buddhahood.

Because it is not about knowing anything, the Zen master's crazy wisdom is beyond logic and language. Zen is about a way of *being*. But if we can't talk about Zen, then how can we talk about Zen?

> Zen is the madman yelling: "If you wanta tell me that the stars are not words, then stop calling them stars!"
>
> JACK KEROUAC

Zen holy fools are out of their minds and want to drive you out of yours. The message in their madness is that their madness is the message.

Zen is not letting yourself be horsewhipped into words about it, so as you read these words just unfocus your eyes and stare at the blurry page.

JACK KEROUAC

If you want to see it, see into it directly; but when you stop to think about it, it is altogether missed.

TAO-WU

We have two eyes to see two sides of things, but there must be a third eye which will see everything at the same time and yet not see anything. That is to understand Zen.

D. T. SUZUKI

The crazy wisdom of the Zen master transforms ordinary experience back into ordinary experience. Most experience is *extra*ordinary, overlaid with our preconceptions and judgments, and filtered through our pragmatic desire to find a *use* for everything. Zen is to move beyond desire, ideas, or words and to experience each moment without qualification. (Now we have more words about what is beyond words.)

Zen holy fools have direct experience of the world from moment to moment, making them capable of continuous spontaneity and playfulness. Zen is perfectly crazy wisdom.

> Master Shih-kung asked the disciple if he could take hold of empty space. The disciple made a grasping movement in the air with his hand but Shih-kung exclaimed, "You got nothing!" The disciple then asked, "What, then, is your way?" Whereupon Shih-kung took hold of the disciple's nose, gave it a sharp twist and called out, "That is the way to take hold of empty space!"
>
> ALAN WATTS
> *The Spirit of Zen*

Form is emptiness and emptiness is form.
PRAJNA PARAMITA SUTRA

We may not be aware of it, but at one time or another, each
of us has probably paid homage to a famous Zen holy fool,
the half-mythical, half-flesh-and-blood character named
Hotai, better known as the Laughing Buddha. He is the pot-
bellied figure whose statue appears in Chinese souvenir shops
and restaurants, who brings good luck if his stomach is
rubbed. His hands are sometimes extended upward as if he
holds up the sky with his crazy dance, and a big silly grin
crosses his broad face. Supposedly, the Laughing Buddha
was modeled after an actual wandering Chinese Zen monk
named Keishi, who some people believe was Maitreya,
another incarnation of Buddha, who arrived unexpectedly in
this jolly, rotund form. By contrast, Gautama, the Buddha
from India who is worshipped worldwide, is traditionally
depicted as trim, handsome, and extremely dignified, with
perfectly symmetrical features and just the slightest of smiles,
as faint as the Mona Lisa's. This sublime smile is one of the
many emblems of the Buddha's spiritual state. A passage in
orthodox Indian Buddhist literature claims that spiritually
advanced people do not laugh out loud and that the most

Everything you do is Zen.
BODHIDHARMA

enlightened will not even show their teeth when they smile. Flying in the face of this stuffy monastic ideal, the folk hero Hotai came along to proclaim that you can be enlightened and still have a belly laugh. You can have great realizations of suffering and emptiness and yet emerge a playful, joyous fat man who drinks a little wine now and then and would rather play hide-and-seek with children all day than chant sutras with a bunch of old monks in a stifling hot temple. The great enlightened wisdom of the formal Buddhist path is not crazy enough for some. In *Zen and the Comic Spirit,* Conrad Hyers writes:

> According to legend Hotai (the laughing Buddha) refused the designation of Zen master, as well as monastic restriction, and instead walked the streets with his sack over his shoulder, giving gifts to children.

The Eastern Crazy Wisdom Poet's Society

The Laughing Buddha symbolizes an entire subculture of crazy wisdom artists, the roaming poet seekers of China and Japan, many of whom were also Taoist or Zen Buddhist monks. This spiritual-poetic subculture spans centuries and includes some of the finest Asian writers and artists. They were usually great lovers of nature and wild places, and many of them became wanderers, living from moment to moment and often from hand to mouth. They shunned official religious institutions, as well as the business of ordinary people, and chose to live free, practicing only their poetry and the art of liberation.

Ryōkan, who lived in the late eighteenth and early nineteenth centuries, is one of the best-known and most beloved figures in Japanese history. He was a wandering crazy wisdom Zen poet who called himself "the Great Fool." Although his enlightenment was certified and he could have become head priest at a temple or monastery, Ryōkan refused any official position and lived in a mountain hermitage. From there he often took long walks through villages where he played with the children and drank sake with the farmers. He preferred the common people over priests, and according to stories, Ryōkan recited his poetry to the villagers whenever asked.

Shaggy hair past the ears
A worn-out robe resembling white clouds and dark
    smoke.

Abandon this fleeting world,
    abandon yourself,
Then the moon and flowers
    will guide you along
    the Way.

RYŌKAN

> Half drunk, half sober, I return home,
> Children all around, guiding me along the Way.

In one of his most celebrated poems, Ryōkan evokes the elusive Zen state of grace, the perfect harmony of simply being.

> With no-mind, blossoms invite the butterfly;
> With no-mind, the butterfly visits the blossoms.
> When the flower blooms, the butterfly comes.
> When the butterfly comes, the flower blooms.
> I do not "know" others.
> Others do not "know" me.
> Not-knowing each other we naturally follow the Way.

Cold Mountain (Han-shan), who named himself after his favorite cliff dwelling, lived in China in the late seventh century during the T'ang dynasty. Cold Mountain was reputed to have great wisdom, and he and his sidekick Pick Up (Shih-te) are now considered "immortals" in Chinese folklore. Cold Mountain and Pick Up worked for a while in the kitchen of a large monastery, and many famous paintings portray these legendary madmen leaning on brooms and laughing uproariously. According to stories about them, they were always singing and clowning around, often making fun of the priests and monks in the region.

Like his Japanese counterpart, Ryōkan, Cold Mountain refused to take any lofty position in a temple or monastery. When a famous priest came to visit him in the kitchen where he worked, Cold Mountain ran away into the mountains and never was seen again. Thereafter he led a hermit's life of poverty and freedom, writing poems on cliffs and stones and pieces of wood.

> I settled at Cold Mountain long ago,
> Already it seems like years and years.
> Freely drifting, I prowl the woods and streams
> And linger watching things themselves.
> Men don't get this far into the mountains,
> White clouds gather and billow.
> Thin grass does for a mattress,
> The blue sky makes a good quilt.
> Happy with a stone underhead
> Let heaven and earth go about their changes.
>
> **COLD MOUNTAIN**

The Moment of Haiku

Japanese haiku poets are like Zen clowns, giving poignant and sometimes humorous glimpses into their bittersweet experience of life. Developed primarily by Japanese Buddhist monks and meditators, haiku marries poetry and Zen by expressing a moment's awareness simply and directly. Just as the great Western spiritual poets Dante and Milton focused their mythopoetic verse through a Christian lens, the poets writing haiku attempt to transcribe their Zen experience. As R. H. Blyth, the scholar of Eastern culture writes, "Haiku is a kind of satori, or enlightenment, in which we see into the life of things."

Haiku is an articulation of the Zen ideal in that it finds the spiritual in the ordinary, saying to us, "Just this." The poet rarely interprets or explains the image or scene being presented, and abstraction or metaphoric flight is usually absent. The aim is to convey one moment's experience, and if the moment contains difficult thoughts or sentiments, the poet simply places these in the context of the haiku, where they become a matter of fact. The personal story is just another aspect of the fleeting scene.

In these latter day
degenerate times,
cherry blossoms everywhere!
ISSA

I leave.
You stay.
Two autumns.

BUSON

A poet writing haiku focuses on a single experience, but often notices two elements—what is perceived in the world and what is perceived in the mind. The poet plays these two perceptions off each other to create poetic tension. Basho, the father of contemporary haiku, calls this interplay "surprising comparison" and describes its effect by saying ". . . the mind goes, and then it comes back again."

The haiku form limits the poet to three lines that total seventeen syllables (in Japanese), requiring great precision of expression. Like the sparse strokes of a Japanese or Chinese ink drawing, a haiku paints a picture and evokes a mood with the fewest of words.

> —the world of dew is only a world of dew
> and yet—
> and yet—
>
> ISSA

Issa is one of the best-loved Japanese haiku poets; like St. Francis of Assisi, he had great affection for all forms of life. In his poetry, Issa often addresses himself to the birds, animals, and insects.

Where there are humans
you'll find flies,
and Buddhas.

ISSA

For you fleas too,
the night must be long,
it must be lonely.

Even among the insects
some can sing,
some can't.

Don't kill the fly!
Look—it's begging you,
Wringing its hands and feet!

O snail
climb Mt. Fuji,
but slowly, slowly!

Issa, like many Asian poets, had great love for the natural world, considering nature a teacher, studying the cycles of birth and death and the ways of other creatures. This led to a long-standing convention, followed in many haiku, that somewhere in each poem there be a reference to a season. These closing haiku are a year's cycle, with one extra for good measure.

People coming, people going
Over the spring moor—
For what, I wonder?

SHIKI

Winter solitude—
In a world of one color
the sound of wind.

BASHO

Ears of my old age;
the summer rains
falling down the rainpipe.

BUSON

The old calendar
Fills me with gratitude,
Like a sutra.

BUSON

Deep autumn;
My neighbor—
How does he live?

BASHO

From the Roof of the World

I see this life as a conjuration and a dream.
Great compassion rises in my heart
For those without a knowledge of this truth.

MILAREPA

The Tibetan Buddhist tradition has produced some great spiritual poets, such as the ascetic Milarepa who taught transcendental wisdom through his improvisational songs. Milarepa chose to live in extreme poverty in the cold of the Himalaya Mountains, mastering himself and the elements at the same time. When a local king sent a messenger to invite him to the royal palace for an audience, Milarepa refused, saying, "I am likewise a mighty king, of the Wheel that Revolveth; and a king who aboundeth in riches is no wise happier or mightier than I."

Milarepa dedicated himself to gaining control over his mind and achieving full enlightenment. He knew this task had nothing to do with wealth or comfort. It also had nothing to do with religion or holy scriptures. As he stated,

> Accustomed long to meditating on the Whispered
>   Chosen Truths,
> I have forgot all that is said in written and printed
>   books.
> Accustomed long to know the meaning of the
>   Wordless,
> I have forgot the way to trace the roots of verbs.
> I have forgot all creeds and dogmas.

Another holy fool of the Himalayas was the rascal Tibetan saint Drukpa Kunley. Through his outrageous behavior, Kunley taught people how to let go of religious formality and be open to all of life. Once, it is told, Kunley came to a village where the people were being very devout, bowing to this virtue or that deity. Kunley chimed in with his own litany:

> I bow to fornicators discontented with their wives;
> I bow to crooked speech and lying talk;
> I bow to ungrateful children;
> I bow to wearers of cloth who break their vows;
> I bow to professors attached to their words;
> I bow to tramps who reject a home;
> I bow to the bums of insatiate whores.

Like many crazy wisdom masters, Kunley made sure
that "sinners" and the poor were included in the realm
of the holy.

CHAPTER 4

Crazy Western Wisdom

In much wisdom is much grief; and he that increaseth knowledge increaseth sorrow.

ECCLESIASTES

The Western expressions of crazy wisdom are more scattered than those of the East and therefore more difficult to trace. Until existentialism appeared in the late nineteenth century, no movement in Western philosophy dealt with the ideas that are so integral to Eastern cultures. Wayward Western philosophers or artists may have arrived at their own understanding, but crazy wisdom has not taken root in the Western psyche or, until recently, been given wide consideration. The reasons for this are deep-rooted.

As we noticed, understanding Eastern crazy wisdom requires a stretch, if not a complete snap, of the Western mind. A Zen poet once remarked, "It is like trying to discuss the color of milk with a blind man." The major difficulty results from disparate attitudes toward reason in the East and the West. Over the centuries Eastern and Western seekers of wisdom have been involved in two somewhat different games of consciousness. Consider the following statements:

Reason is the true self of every man, since it is the supreme and better part.

ARISTOTLE

Stop thinking, and end your problems.
LAO-TZU

A kind of East-West split exists in the world psyche. It seems that the planet is divided in much the same way as the brain: into two hemispheres, each with its own methods for understanding. Broadly speaking, Eastern and Western seekers of wisdom have taken two fundamentally different approaches.

Virtue is knowledge.
PLATO

If you try to know it, you have already departed from it.
CHUANG-TZU

Early on in their experiments with consciousness, Eastern sages, seeking inner peace, attempted to gain control over their thoughts and emotions. As they gazed inward they discovered the intellect to be an unreliable and often treacherous tool, the agent of our alienation. They began to understand that the rational mind, although important to survival, can dislocate us from ourselves and the rest of creation.

Oriental man remains intuitive, not rational. The lifting of reason out of the primeval waters of the unconscious is a Greek achievement.

WILLIAM BARRETT

In another part of the planet, the Western seekers of wisdom, beginning with the Greeks, became infatuated with the rational mind. Their belief in the mind's supremacy placed humans above the rest of creation and fostered in the Western psyche an intense identification with the individual self or "soul". The Western enterprise came to center on developing the intellect and strengthening the self as a way of knowing and controlling the world.

A fair amount of crazy wisdom is nevertheless concealed within the dominant Western view. A few holy fools have infiltrated the mainstream Judeo-Christian-Islamic traditions, and some have even been sanctified or afforded the status of hero, but usually only after their death. Like their Taoist and Zen counterparts, the Western holy fools attempt to lose themselves in union with all of creation, but they usually have an agent, an intervening presence called God or Christ or Mohammed. And whereas many Eastern masters emphasize unity with the *ordinary* nature of things, the Jewish, Christian, and Muslim mystics instead seek something extraordinary. They yearn for *ecstatic* union, full of flames and visions and all manner of special effects.

Like all crazy wisdom masters, the holy fools of the West made up their own spiritual practices. They usually left the churches and temples behind, heading off alone to the desert, or to the slums and shtetls to live with the poor. They knew that true wisdom was rarely found in institutions or in proximity to the wealthy and worldly-wise.

> The world is ruled by letting things take their course.
> LAO-TZU

Fools for Christ

In the fourth century A.D., the first Christian hermits left their churches for the desert sands, the sparse landscape where Jesus and Moses had found truth and where Western holy fools have often had visions. These fervent individuals, who came to be known as the "desert fathers," were willing to pay a lonely, burning price for their own experience of the divine.

> Blessed Macarius said: This is the truth, if a monk regards contempt as praise, poverty as riches, and hunger as a feast, he will never die.
>
> THOMAS MERTON
> *Wisdom of the Desert*

The desert fathers attempted to diminish themselves through austerity until they became one with the divine. In the stillness and solitude of the desert, they sought unity with all creation. Like the Eastern sages, the desert fathers believed that language, and in particular scripture, was inadequate for either promoting or explaining spiritual experience.

> When Abbot Pambo was asked to say a few words to the very important Bishop of Alexandria, who was visiting some of the Desert Fathers, the elder replied: "If he is not edified by my silence, there is no hope that he will be edified by my words."
>
> THOMAS MERTON
> *Wisdom of the Desert*

St. Francis of Assisi was an early thirteen-century mystic who lived crazy wisdom completely. After his sudden enlightenment he stripped naked and renounced his inheritance, declaring himself forever after "married to Lady Poverty."

In 1209 Francis founded his order of "little brothers" who sought union with God through abstinence and poverty. The extreme behavior and appearance of his early followers apparently embarrassed the church, and finally a local bishop asked Francis to take them off the streets and find decent clothes and housing for them. Francis refused, explaining, "If we had possessions we would need weapons for their defense."

Francis is remembered for his gentle nature and his love for all creatures. According to legend, after a rainstorm he would pick up the earthworms, removing them from the streets so they would not be stepped on. The Order of the Little Brothers was widely known for their joyous and playful ways, and Francis referred to himself and his followers as "jesters of the Lord."

Righteous Ones

Alas! The world is full of enormous lights and mysteries, and man shuts them from himself with one small hand!

THE BAAL SHEM TOV
IN *Tales of the Hasidim* BY MARTIN BUBER

Many Hasidic rabbis fit into the crazy wisdom canon, most notably the founder of Hasidism, the Baal Shem Tov— the "possessor of the good name." Like so many holy fools, the Baal Shem Tov was a hero of the poor and oppressed. His flock consisted of Eastern European Jewish peasants who lived in the early eighteenth century during the pogrom years. The Baal Shem Tov and his later Hasidic disciples rejected elitism and the intellectual squabbles of rabbinical schools, teaching that the simplest people and prayers were God's favorites. The Baal Shem Tov claimed that:

> The lowest of the low you can think of, is dearer to me than your only son is to you.

While most of Judaism merely waited for the Messiah's return to be delivered from woes and oppression, the Baal Shem Tov taught people to live in the moment, with great energy and joy. "If I love God," he asked, "what need have I of a coming world?" He showed his followers the "sparks of God in all things," and like St. Francis, he talked to animals and trees. However, in *Tales of the Hasidim*, Martin Buber tells of one tree that the Baal Shem Tov avoided.

> It is said that once, when all souls were gathered together in Adam's soul, at the very moment in which he stood poised beside the Tree of Knowledge, the soul of the Baal Shem got up and left, and did not eat of the fruit of the tree.

The Baal Shem Tov was one of the zaddikim, a line of rabbis known as the "righteous ones." These rabbis were a
forceful influence, much like the Eastern Zen masters who,
after having an experience of enlightenment, helped others
arrive at their own. Like their Asian counterparts, the zaddikim rarely preached, and instead transmitted wisdom
through parables and riddles, or through singing and dancing. Often they were living examples of crazy wisdom—
they taught by being. One Hasidic student tells how he
came to know the holy book: "I learned the Torah from
all the limbs of my teacher."

Whirling Words: The Poetry of Rumi

Give up owning things and being somebody.
Quit existing.

RUMI

Out of the thirteenth-century Islamic world danced
Mavlana (The Awakened One) Jelaluddin Rumi, one of
the world's greatest spiritual poets. Rumi is revered by

millions, especially throughout the Muslim nations where devotees are often heard chanting his poetry, which is considered by some to be second in importance only to the Koran. Rumi founded one of the most influential Sufi brotherhoods, an order that emphasized music and whirling dancing as the path to awakening. The members of Rumi's order came to be known as dervishes.

> All the atoms in the air and in the desert,
> Let it be known, are like madmen.
> Each atom, happy or miserable,
> Is in love with the Sun of which we can say nothing.

Much of Rumi's verse was created in an improvisational manner, the spontaneous combustion of a spirit on fire, transcribed by followers as they listened to him speak in pure song. Rumi's legacy includes the *Divan*, a volume with forty-two thousand lines of poetry, and the *Mathnawi*, his masterwork, a six-volume collection of stories, aphorisms, jokes, and over fifty-one thousand verses.

Although he was a master of words, Rumi always looked beyond them; neither language nor knowledge was as important as his love of the divine. Like his Asian counterparts, Rumi refused official recognition as a wise man.

The people here want to put me in charge. They want me to be Judge, Magistrate, and Interpreter of all the texts. The Knowing I have doesn't want that. It wants to enjoy itself. I am a plantation of sugarcane, and at the same time I'm eating the sweetness.

Knowledge that is acquired is not like this. Those who have it worry if audiences like it or not. It's a bait for popularity. Disputational knowing wants customers. It has no soul. Robust and energetic before a responsive crowd, it slumps when no one is there.

The only real customer is God. Chew quietly your sweet sugarcane God-Love, and stay playfully childish. Your face will turn rosy with illumination like the rose-bud flowers.

The Sacred Clowns

Another brand of Western crazy wisdom comes through the sacred clowns of the Native American tribes. These clowns appear at religious ceremonies, usually with sex on their minds and outsized phalli between their legs. They disrupt the solemn proceedings and sometimes lead special bawdy rituals of their own.

In his book, *Technicians of the Sacred*, Jerome Rothenberg describes a Cherokee ritual called the "Booger

Event." Sacred clowns—"the boogers"—enter the ritual circle and begin breaking wind and making foul noises. Each booger has an obscene name, such as Big Balls, Asshole, Rusty Asshole, Burster, Swollen Pussy, Sweet Prick, or Piercer. Once inside the circle, the boogers act like madmen, falling on the ground, and pushing at the male spectators as if to get at their wives and daughters. After a while, the boogers begin to dance. Each booger's name is taken in turn as the first word of a song that is sung while that booger dances a solo, using awkward, grotesque steps. The audience applauds each mention of his name, while the other dancers thrust out their buttocks and occasionally display the large phalli concealed under their clothing. These phalli may contain water, which is sprayed on the spectators. Finally, female dancers enter the circle to be the boogers' partners. As soon as they do, the boogers increase their sexual exhibitions, closing in on the women from behind and gyrating in simulated sexual intercourse.

Christian missionaries must have been shocked to witness such events, especially as part of a religious ceremony. While many Christians regard it as unfortunate that our spirits are forced to dwell in wild, smelly animal bodies, these "sacred clowns" reveled in their physical incarnation.

The sacred clown can be found in other cultures as well. The priests who led the revelry at Greek Dionysian festivals were a sect of sacred clowns—blessing sex, intoxication, and madness in the struggle against Apollonian forces of reason. A sacred clown played a part in the solemn Greek pilgrimage from Athens to Eleusis, a route lined with temples. On a bridge over the river Kephissos, a clown waited to make obscene gestures and curse at the pilgrims. We can only surmise the intent, but perhaps the clown was there to humble worshippers and remind them of their human nature as they went to meet the gods.

A slightly different breed of sacred clown made an appearance in medieval Europe leading the Feast of Fools. A procession of revelers and masqueraders marched into a church, sang obscene songs, told dirty jokes, sprayed the congregation with smelly "holy water," and burned incense made from old shoe leather or cow dung. This riotous annual ritual took place inside Catholic churches, even under the vaults of Notre-Dame de Paris. The church sanctioned this travesty for a while, and sometimes the clergy even participated by electing the leader of the revelers, who was called "the Fools' Pope." Eventually the church forced this "mass" into the streets, where it found expression in Carnival and New Year's Eve.

A similar group of jesters presided over the *festum asinarium,* a strange ritual mass in medieval Catholic churches commemorating Mary's flight into Egypt. During this ceremony asses were led into the church and, after each element of the mass, the congregation responded with donkey sounds. Let us bray?

The rituals of all these Western sacred clowns seem to compromise an acknowledgment of nature and the animal, both around us and within us. Though officially squelched by the one on high, our wild, natural urges demanded a place of honor and a means of expression. Sacred clowns make no distinction between high and low, the sacred and the profane, and they won't let us forget that we have only recently stood upright and put on these garments.

CHAPTER 5

The Existential Get Down

> I want everything to be explained to me or nothing.
> And the reason is impotent when it hears this cry from
> the heart. The mind aroused by this insistence seeks
> and finds nothing but contradictions and nonsense.
> The world itself, whose single meaning I do not under-
> stand, is a vast irrational.
>
> ALBERT CAMUS

It was intelligence and nothing else that had to be opposed.

SOREN AABYE KIERKEGAARD

Our reason has driven all away. Alone at last, we end up by ruling over a desert.

ALBERT CAMUS

In the eighteenth and nineteenth centuries, after a long history of brow-wrinkling, brain-twisting, mind-sweating reason, Western thinkers came to the bitter conclusion that the intellect could not comprehend the world or its meaning. Not long thereafter the movement known as existentialism pronounced the failure of reason and the death of classical Western philosophy. Something new was necessary.

The existentialists practiced crazy wisdom by challenging both God and reason, and thus the Western claim of humanity's special place in creation. We were no longer the chosen ones, watched over like children by a beneficent God, our Father, nor was intellect deemed capable of discovering truth or finding higher meaning for our lives. These conclusions, along with the work of Darwin and Freud, shattered the Western psyche. The individual mind and soul—the darlings of Occidental philosophy and religion—were no longer the centerpieces of creation, and it became the grim project of the existentialists to mourn their passing and write the elegies.

> Forever I shall be a stranger to myself. In psychology as in logic, there are truths but no truth. Socrates' "Know thyself" has as much value as the "Be virtuous" of our confessionals. They reveal a nostalgia at the same time as an ignorance.
>
> ALBERT CAMUS

Like tricksters, the existentialists attempted to overturn the moral codes and belief systems of their time, but they too became victims of the resulting confusion. Unlike the Taoists and Zen Buddhists, many existentialists were driven into severe depression by their inability to find meaning in the world. The effect on them is revealed in the titles of their books: *Nausea, Fear and Trembling, The Concept of Dread, No Exit.*

The Way of the Absurd

The existentialists referred to a meaningless life and world as being "absurd." Confronted with an "absurd creation," Albert Camus wrote of the "absurd man" who must find a different approach to life and another mode of understanding:

The world can no longer offer anything to the man filled with anguish.

MARTIN HEIDEGGER

With God dead, there remains only history and power.

ALBERT CAMUS

> For the absurd man it is not a matter of explaining
> and solving, but of experiencing and describing.
> Everything begins with lucid indifference.

Any Eastern sage would be pleased with Camus's phrase "lucid indifference," which sounds similar to the just being of Zen or the deliberate nondoing of Taoism. However, unlike the Taoist at peace with the Tao, Camus himself never made peace with the absurd. He was well aware of his dilemma:

> If I were a tree among trees, a cat among animals,
> this life would have a meaning, or rather this problem
> would not arise, for I should belong to this world. I
> should *be* this world to which I am now opposed by
> my whole consciousness and my whole insistence
> upon familiarity. This ridiculous reason is what sets
> me in opposition to all creation. I cannot cross it out
> with a stroke of the pen.

Camus wanted out of his mind and into just being. But no Taoist or Zen master was around to give Camus lessons; there was no tradition in the West to accommodate his yearnings, no methods to transform his existentialism into a way of life. He was a man of philosophy, and when the thinking game failed him, he sank into despair.

Of all the existentialists, the nineteenth century philosopher Friedrich Nietzsche may be the most deserving of the title crazy wisdom master, as evidenced by this poem:

> I live in my own place
> have never copied nobody even half,
> and at any master who lacks the grace
> to laugh at himself—I laugh.
>
> INSCRIBED OVER THE DOOR TO NIETZSCHE'S HOUSE

Nietzsche developed his own unique crazy wisdom philosophy, which has a great deal in common with both the ideas and presentation of the Eastern sages. There are moments when Nietzsche, explaining his wild, anarchist beliefs, sounds exactly like an old Taoist holy fool:

> All that is good is instinct—and hence easy, necessary, free. Laboriousness is an objection; the god is typically different from the hero. (In my language: light feet are the first attribute of divinity.)

Nietzsche's divine "light feet" are right in step with the Taoists, but his own heavy boots would not allow him to walk quite so softly. Instead, he felt it necessary to kick apart the foundations of European civilization. With a trickster's chaotic spirit and a jester's skeptical insights, Nietzsche took it on himself to destroy all previous Western thought and history. In this task, he saw himself as the great fool philosopher, a crazy wisdom prophet come to herald a new age.

> It seems to me more and more that the philosopher, as a *necessary* man of tomorrow and the day after tomorrow, has always found himself, and always had to find himself, in opposition to his today: the ideal of the day was always his enemy. . . . Each time [the real philosopher] said: "We must proceed there, that way, where today you are least at home."

Nietzsche believed that truth is found in "being" rather than knowing, but like Camus, he had no one to teach him how to *be*. He comes very close to Zen when he refuses to search for truth, and decides to have breakfast instead.

> The "true" world—an idea which is no longer good for anything, not even obligating—an idea which has become useless and superfluous—*consequently*, a refuted idea: let us abolish it! (Bright day; breakfast; return of *bon sens* and cheerfulness; Plato's embarrassed blush; pandemonium of all free spirits.)

Like most crazy wisdom masters, Nietzsche saw the human craving for knowledge and significance as our most distressing quality, keeping us grim and out of balance.

> Gradually, man has become a fantastic animal that has to fulfill one more condition of existence than any other animal: man *has* to believe, to know, from time to time *why* he exists; his race cannot flourish without a periodic trust in life—without faith in *reason in life*. And again and again the human race will decree from time to time: "There is something at which it is absolutely forbidden to laugh."

Nietzsche summarized his understanding with a statement that could also be considered the perilous credo of modernity: "The advantages of our time: nothing is true, everything is permitted." However, in the end, Jean-Paul Sartre may have best summarized the difficult existential position, as well as the previous two millennia of Western philosophy with this simple assertion:

> Being has not been given its due.

CHAPTER 6

The Art of Crazy Wisdom

> There is the poet to whom the muse dictates his chants, there is the artist whose hand is guided by an unknown being using him as an instrument. Their reason cannot impede them, they never struggle, and their work shows no signs of strain. They are not divine and can do without their selves. They are like prolongations of nature, and their works do not pass through the intellect.
>
> GUILLAUME APOLLINAIRE

The Art of Being

From the first human who picked up a stick to beat out a rhythm on a log or draw an animal's picture in the dirt, artists have given name and form to the mysteries. As agents of the Tao, or Jesus, or "the absurd," artists show us the latest version of the truth. They make wisdom dance.

The crazy wisdom artist cuts off one ear to clear the eyes for painting, wails down the walls of oppression with a ram's-horn saxophone, dances until the body becomes spirit, sits in a New York garret or on a Chinese mountaintop and writes poetry to the wind or the next lost generation, tells stories constantly, and sings to us of other truths, crying, "Look! This too is how it is."

Artists employ all the archetypal crazy wisdom disguises. As clowns they transform their bewilderment or innocent wonder into art; as tricksters they reveal our shadow nature, stepping boldly into the realms of sex, chaos, and death; as jesters they parody fashions and beliefs. However, the greatest artists are great fools. As the great fool, an artist transforms us, brings us back to our senses by opening our eyes and ears to another reality, or to *this* reality—the world around us that we ordinarily don't see.

> The poet is he who, beneath the named, constantly expected differences, rediscovers the buried kinship between things, the scattered resemblances.
>
> MICHEL FOUCAULT
> *The Order of Things*

Artists are often agents of crazy wisdom. They speak to a different part of us, bypassing the cloudy filter of reason and the fears and prejudices of the habitual mind. They are visited by the Muses, or tormented by their own passions and demons. By translating their inner turmoil or understanding into art, they challenge the accepted notions of reality and create new ones.

If the world were clear, art would not exist.

ALBERT CAMUS

If I could tell you what it
meant, there would be no
point in dancing it.

ISADORA DUNCAN

Like Zen, most art does not take well to definition.
As Louis Armstrong replied when asked to define jazz,
"Man, if you gotta ask, you'll never know."

James Joyce formulated a theory of art that defined
the artistic experience as "aesthetic arrest." According to
Joyce, art does not have purpose; it exists neither to teach
nor to motivate. In the purest sense, art simply captures
rhythms or relationships, immersing us in the moment
and producing an effect not much different from the Zen
master's shout or blow.

> Art is frozen Zen.
>
> R. H. BLYTH

Albert Camus's existential theory of art also sounds like a
Zen master's aesthetic. For Camus, the artist embodies us
in the world and in the moment—with particulars, with
stories, with things.

> The true work of art is always on the human scale.
> It is essentially the one that says, "less."

As Camus saw it, art can teach us what science and reason cannot. In opposition to Plato, Camus believed we can know the world through the body and the senses.

> The work of art is born of the intelligence's refusal to reason the concrete. It marks the triumphs of the carnal.

Great artists stop the mind; their work brings a sudden, intuitive revelation that allows the subconscious or the superconscious to come to the forefront. Like spiritual crazy wisdom masters, artists enlighten us or lighten us up. They teach us how to "be." They give us playthings, plays, play.

> Theater takes place all the time, wherever one is, and art simply facilitates persuading one that this is the case.
>
> JOHN CAGE

Aesthetics is for the artists as ornithology is for the birds.
BARNETT NEWMAN

Meaningless Play

We have art in order not to perish of truth.

FRIEDRICH NIETZSCHE

While the absurd drove most existential philosophers crazy or left them trembling in their lofts, artists began to play with meaninglessness, discovering shapes that might be made from the void. At the beginning of the twentieth century, the philosophic-artistic movements of Dadaism, Futurism, and Surrealism turned the absurd into art— "in order not to perish of truth."

> Let's break away from rationality as out of a horrible husk and throw ourselves like pride-spiced fruit into the immense distorted mouth of the wind! Let's give ourselves up to the unknown, not out of desperation but to plumb the deep pits of the absurd.
>
> F. T. MARTINETTI
> *The Foundation and Manifesto of Futurism,* 1908

Like great tricksters, the early-twentieth-century artists decided to put a grin on the face of the absurd. They sought symbolic representations of the new ethos, a way to honor "being" itself, even if life had no ultimate meaning. Dadaism and Surrealism made acceptance of the absurd a point of honor for the brave, those who could live with, and even rejoice in, a godless and purposeless universe. André Breton wrote:

> I believe in the pure Surrealist joy of the man who, forewarned that all others before him have failed, refuses to admit defeat, sets off from whatever point he chooses, along any other path save a reasonable one, and arrives wherever he can.

Twentieth-century artists made a complete break with Western tradition, renouncing previous values and aesthetic standards. They discovered the freedom, foretold by Nietzsche, to create new realities, and to revel in the energy of existence. They also had a good time kicking in the windows of old institutions.

> We will destroy museums, libraries, and fight against moralism . . . and all utilitarian cowardice. We are on the extreme promontory of ages! Why look back since we must break down the mysterious doors of Impossibility? Time and Space died yesterday.

> We already live in the Absolute for we have already
> created the omnipresent eternal speed.
>
> F. T. MARTINETTI
> *The Foundation and Manifesto of Futurism,* 1908

The artists of the early twentieth century brought the philosophy of existentialism to life. They turned solid shapes into liquid ones, distorted human forms and faces, took apart words and their meanings, and gave creation a new name—Dada.

Dada and Tao

> The great mystery is a secret, but it's known to a few
> people. They will never say what dada is.
>
> TRISTAN TZARA

Out of the imagination of some early-twentieth-century artists came a madcap, multidimensional demigod known as Dada, which bears an uncanny resemblance to the Tao. The Dadaist movement was founded in Zurich during World War I by the French poet and self-proclaimed "literary terrorist" Tristan Tzara. Although Dadaist poetry and

manifestos often sound like a takeoff on the Tao, we have
no evidence that Tzara or other Dadaists were acquainted
with Taoist writings. Perhaps a mysterious transmission
took place.

> Dada is a quantity of life in transparent, effortless,
> and gyratory transformation.
>
> TRISTAN TZARA

> Tao never does anything;
> Yet through it all things are done.
>
> LAO-TZU, FIFTH CENTURY B.C.

Dada and the Tao (which is pronounced "Dao") seem to
do the same dance, perhaps as partners, separated only by
time. Even the letters in the name proclaim a relationship.
Tao and Dada. Tzu and Tzara. The crazy wisdom likeness
goes deeper.

> Logic is a complication. Logic is always false. DADA
> suggests 2 solutions: NO MORE LOOKS! NO MORE
> WORDS! Stop looking! Stop talking!
>
> TRISTAN TZARA

Those who know don't talk.
Those who talk don't know.

LAO-TZU

Dada may be a Western twentieth-century name for the Tao. Or else it is not that at all. Maybe it is just Dada.

DADA is a virgin microbe
DADA is against the high cost of living
DADA
limited company for the exploitation of ideas
DADA has 391 different attitudes and colours
   according to the sex
of the president
It changes—affirms—says the opposite at the same
   time—no
importance—shouts—goes fishing.
Dada is the chameleon of rapid and self-interested
   change.
Dada is against the future. Dada is dead. Dada is
   absurd.
   Long
live Dada. Dada is not a literary school, howl

TRISTAN TZARA
"Dada Manifesto on Feeble Love and Bitter Love"

The similarities between Tao and Dada include the fact that they both appear to be names for everything. Furthermore, like the Tao, Dada makes no distinctions—no high and low, no holy and profane. The Tao and Dada also point to a similar way of living.

> The acts of life have neither beginning nor end.
> Everything happens in a very idiotic fashion.
> That's why everything is the same. Simplicity is
>   called dada.
>
> TRISTAN TZARA

> Approach it and there is no beginning;
> follow it and there is no end.
> You can't know it, but you can be it,
> At ease in your own life.
>
> LAO-TZU

John Cage and the Music of Sound

John Cage's music, like Tzara's Dada, shows us that everything is equal—and equally unimportant. In 1952, in response to a request for a manifesto on music, Cage wrote:

> instantaneous and unpredictable
> nothing is accomplished by writing a piece of music
> nothing is accomplished by hearing a piece of music
> nothing is accomplished by playing a piece of music
> our ears are now in excellent condition

John Cage is an exemplary crazy wisdom artist who became one of the twentieth century's most influential cultural figures. His unusual classical music compositions led to the development of "happenings," events in which the audience participates or there is some convergence of art and ordinary life. An author and lecturer, Cage is very articulate about his motivations and techniques. If his art has any purpose, he says, it is to help us "become fluent with the life we are living."

> I'm not really trying to say anything in my music.
> I hope the music becomes an example, an instance that bridges more or less naturally to the absence of music. So that either you have the music or you don't have it and in either case you have sounds. Hopefully, then people can learn to become attentive, with pleasure, to the world of sounds around us that are changing all the time.

Cage denies the significance of music and rejects the idea that music is something separate from other sounds. Like a great fool, Cage hears a universe full of music that is inaudible to the rest of us. Since he makes no distinction between good and bad sounds, everything becomes music— a never-ending unfinished symphony. Cage wants to share his music with us, but first we must be liberated from our habits of hearing and our tired ideas about music, art, and ultimately, life. He writes:

> If you develop an ear for sounds that are musical it is like developing an ego. You begin to refuse sounds that are not musical and that way cut yourself off from a good deal of experience.

Cage hears continuous music: a modulating concerto of bird songs, car engines, shuffling feet, white noise, commercials, wind, rustling paper—all writing themselves into the random mix. He states:

> My favorite piece of music is the one we hear all the time if we are quiet.

At least one performance of a Cage piano piece produced no intentional sound at all: the pianist made a grand entrance and sat down at the piano, but did not once touch the keys during the entire performance. The only "music" was the incidental sounds of an auditorium full of people, shuffling, coughing, and whispering. Cage also wrote a composition for instruments that can be found in an ordinary living room, and one that uses radios turned on to whatever is being broadcast at the time. He is a musical trickster offering us the revelations of a great fool.

Verses of Crazy Wisdom

Man fixes some wonderful erection of his own between himself and the wild chaos, and gradually goes bleached and stifled under his parasol. Then comes a poet, enemy of convention, and makes a slit in the umbrella; and lo! the glimpse of chaos is a vision, a window to the sun.

D. H. LAWRENCE

You dream you are the doer,
You dream that action is done,
You dream that action bears
    fruit
It is your ignorance,
It is the world's delusion
That gives you these dreams.

BHAGAVAD GITA

Poets are crazy wisdom's children, and poetry is the medium through which crazy wisdom states its case. Lao-tzu, the preacher of the Book of Ecclesiastes, and the storyteller of the Bhagavad Gita were poets of the highest order. They wrote the scriptures of crazy wisdom in verse.

Poets often find their visions to be in opposition to their era, and their poetic voices are shaped by that tension. The European Romantic poets of the late eighteenth and early nineteenth centuries proclaimed that the Western mind and heart were out of balance. They saw the cold, objective intellect as the driving force behind the Industrial Revolution, which was already threatening the natural world. These poets also warned that reason and knowledge can suffocate the "romantic" spirit—the mystical bond between an individual and the rest of creation. In counterpoint to the Age of Reason and the Industrial Revolution, these poets sang of nature, subjective experience, and the powers of imagination.

One of the most radical and prophetic voices of the eighteenth century was that of William Blake. He rejected reason's authority in matters of reality, and the church's authority in matters of morality. He constructed his own mythical universe, in which evil is called "Urizen" (your reason), and the church is portrayed as the destroyer of energy and joy.

> I must Create a System or be enslav'd by another Man's. I will not Reason and Compare; my business is to Create.
>
> WILLIAM BLAKE

> The Errors of a Wise Man make your Rule Rather than the Perfections of a Fool.
>
> WILLIAM BLAKE

All Bibles or sacred codes have been the causes of
the following Errors:

1. That Man has two real existing principles: Viz:
   a Body and a Soul.
2. That Energy, call'd Evil, is alone from the Body; &
   that Reason, call'd Good, is alone from the Soul.
3. That God will torment Man in Eternity for following his Energies.

Blake received little recognition from his contemporaries
and was considered a minor poet or madman by those who
read him. Today he is widely quoted and regarded as a
visionary. It is the story of many a master of crazy wisdom.

He has observ'd the Golden Rule
Till he's become the Golden Fool.

WILLIAM BLAKE

America's Beat poets confronted an advanced stage of the
same civilization opposed by the Romantics. The Beats
tried to break through the self-satisfied consumerism and
reasonableness that held sway over American society from
the late 1940s through the early 1960s. In the brash dialect
of the streets, the Beats hurled their crazy wisdom verses at
the Establishment. They were just a few lonely voices,

courageous in their indictment of a society strangled by conformity, a nation blinded to its imperial evils. In a poem called "Death to Van Gogh's Ear!" written in 1958, Allen Ginsberg decried the state of the nation:

> Poet is Priest
> Money has reckoned the soul of America
> Congress broken thru to the precipice of Eternity
> The President built a War machine which will vomit and
> rear up Russia out of Kansas
> The American Century betrayed by a mad Senate
>   which no
> longer sleeps with its wife

Beat poets drew their inspiration from many sources, but a few—including Gary Snyder, Allen Ginsberg, and Jack Kerouac—were influenced heavily by their contact with Taoism and Buddhism. They began to translate the crazy wisdom of Eastern sages into an American idiom.

> The reason why there are so many things
> Is because the mind breaks it up,
> The shapes are empty
> That sprung into come
> But the mind won't know this

Till a Buddha with a golden
Lighted finger, hath pointed
To the thumb, & made an aphorism
In a robe on the street,
That you'll know what it means
For there be too many things
In a world of no-thing.

JACK KEROUAC

Gary Snyder was deeply influenced by the Taoists and Zen Buddhists. He studied Buddhism for many years in Japan, and later founded a Zen meditation community in the Sierra foothills. In the 1960s, long before the environment became a mainstream concern, Snyder was attempting to awaken people to the interdependence of all life and the intrinsic value of wilderness. He wrote:

"From the masses to the masses" the most
Revolutionary consciousness is to be found
Among the most ruthlessly exploited classes:
Animals, trees, water, air, grasses.

The Beat poets, to whom "beat" meant beatitude, were considered cranks and delinquents by most social and literary critics of the period. In recent years, however, a few Beat poets have been awarded literary prizes, and mainstream society has acknowledged their writings and causes. If the Beats had lived in an earlier century, they would have been honored only posthumously, like so many poets throughout history, but the speed of twentieth-century cultural transformation revealed them as crazy wisdom prophets within their own lifetimes.

CHAPTER 7

How to Become Crazy and Wise

How does crazy wisdom happen? What gyre of gene or bug of brain produces crazy wisdom in an individual? Is it born in the blood, or can it be learned? Where does crazy wisdom get its insights into human behavior and its vast perspectives on the cosmos? If crazy wisdom knows that we don't know, then how does crazy wisdom know *that*?

> What we need is a good five-cent synthesis.
>
> SAUL BELLOW

Modern science may have discovered the seat of crazy wisdom in the right hemisphere of our cerebral cortex. Recent research has found that the human brain's two hemispheres tend to have separate functions and modes of operation. The left hemisphere seems to be in charge of logic, mathematics, and ordinary language activities, while the right hemisphere controls kinesthesis, artistic sensibility, and special judgment. The left hemisphere is the business center, the place where we work to survive. The right hemisphere is existential, the place where we live and love. The left gets us where we are going, the right puts us in touch with where we are.

Long before we understood the function of each hemisphere, it was recognized that people have at least

May God us keep
From single vision and
Newton's sleep.

WILLIAM BLAKE

two modes of understanding. Philosopher Thomas Hobbes called one mode "directed" and the other "free." Indian spiritual teacher Radhakrishanan called one "rational" and the other "integral." French anthropologist Claude Lévi-Strauss referred to one as "positive" and the other as "mythic." A graphic and poetic description of the "two minds" appears in the second-century Indian Buddhist text, the Lankavatara Sutra:

> The discriminating mind is a dancer and a magician with the objective world as his stage. Intuitive mind is the wise jester who travels with the magician and reflects upon his emptiness and transiency.

The left hemisphere is the utilitarian brain, the opposable thumb of the mind. It receives information, analyzes the world, gives out names (dog, god, grass, open, gone), and arranges sensory input in familiar patterns. The left hemisphere is an information processor, working bit by bit in a linear, sequential manner.

The right hemisphere's primary function is synthesis, seeing relationships between things and providing an overview. The right hemisphere has been called holistic in

The left brain is a scientist, the right is an artist.
COLIN WILSON

O to be delivered from the
rational into the realm of
pure song . . .

THEODORE ROETHKE

its vision and intuitive in its operation. This part of the
brain connects the dots . . . but doesn't count them.

One key to understanding the right hemisphere can
be found in its association with music and poetry. Studies
have shown that people with left-hemisphere brain damage
who have lost most of their language ability can still use
words, but only to sing songs that they learned before the
damage. Other patients start writing and speaking in
poetry for the first time.

The right hemisphere seems to control awareness of
the body. Patients with right-hemisphere brain damage are
sometimes unable to dress themselves, though their speech
and reasoning abilities are intact. Perhaps one of the functions of the right hemisphere is to bring us down from the
abstract world of words and ideas and put us back into
our bodies, giving us a sense of our physical presence on
the earth.

Our culture's ontological prejudice is obvious from
the attitude of medical science toward brain injuries. If only
the right hemisphere is damaged and no injury has occurred
to language or logic functions, doctors often consider it
"minor" brain damage. Perhaps the heavy emphasis on
analysis during medical school has left some doctors a bit

lopsided, understanding the brain primarily through their own left hemispheres. As Robert Ornstein states in his classic study, *The Psychology of Consciousness,* this lopsidedness has broader and more disturbing implications:

> . . . the development of a hyperanalytic, "rational" science, unchecked by a comprehensive understanding born of intuition, can develop into the destruction of all on the planet.

It is obvious that something is not working properly. How else can we explain our mismanagement of resources and of our own population, the pollution and destruction of our environment, or the mass murder of our own species? We cannot see the bigger picture and how we fit into it. We are no longer in our bodies; we are not in our right minds. Ornstein sees the problem this way:

> A shift toward a comprehensive consciousness of the interconnectedness of life, toward a relinquishing of the "every man for himself" attitude inherent in our ordinary construction of consciousness, might enable us to take those "selfless" steps that could begin to solve our collective problems. Certainly our culture has too severely emphasized the development of only one way of organizing reality.

Mr. Duffy lived a short distance from his body.
JAMES JOYCE
Ulysses

Perhaps the crises threatening humanity in our time arises from a simple functional imbalance, an unequal distribution of strength between the brain's left and right hemispheres. Maybe we need a little electrical work, a rewiring of the cerebral circuits. Perhaps exercising the right hemisphere through techniques such as meditation, or exposure to art, music, and nature might bring us a new sanity or consciousness and a more integrated way of living.

Some adventurous cultural anthropologists believe that the recent emergence of mysticism, feminism, and deep ecology are the species' attempt to regain equilibrium. Our survival instinct may be telling us to reawaken our more receptive modes of understanding. Even obsession with sex, drugs, and rock and roll may be seen as an attempt to find relief from the oppression of the rational, controlling mind. A new and necessary mutation may be taking place, attempting to correct the cultural and evolutionary imbalances of the past few thousand years.

There is no way to know what will happen to our species, but while we wait for the verdict, crazy wisdom is hanging out in the right hemisphere. Being on the right side of the brain is a little like being on the Left Bank in Paris: relaxing while watching the passing show, listening to the

> All Things want to fly. Only *we* are weighed down by desire, caught in ourselves and enthralled with our heaviness. . . . If someone were to fall into intimate slumber, and slept deeply with Things—how easily he would come to a different day, out of the mutual depth.
>
> RAINER MARIA RILKE

music on the corner. It's a place to sit around and tell stories and wonder about it all—and most important, to slow down. Call it crazy or lazy, this wisdom may be found only by slowing down and learning the art of being. As Carl Jung explains, this is much more difficult than it sounds:

> We must be able to let things happen in the psyche. For us, this actually is an art of which few people know anything. Consciousness is forever interfering, helping, correcting, and negating, and never leaving the simple growth of the psychic processes in peace. It would be simple enough, if only simplicity were not the most difficult of all things.

Pigments and Pinecones

Crazy wisdom can be awakened through experiences involving art or nature, although in both of these realms the process is somewhat mysterious. It *does* seem clear that the transformative qualities of a symphony or sunset engage the nonrational, intuitive mode of understanding.

The experience of art, as discussed earlier, can clear a path for crazy wisdom. Through Joyce's "aesthetic arrest" or Camus's "triumph of the carnal," the artist can bypass reason and give us a different sense of ourselves, embodying us in the world. Art can also offer perspective, showing us the wider contexts in which we live.

Nature also places us in the larger context: The sky and mountains and oceans are capable of dwarfing or drowning us. Sometimes they take our breath away along with our self-importance. Robinson Jeffers, whose choice of nature over man was a lifelong poetic theme, expressed this moment of transcendent understanding.

> For it's not innocent blank nature made hills look sad and woe-y, it's men, with their awful minds . . .
>
> JACK KEROUAC

> The sea's voice worked into my mood, I thought "no matter
> What happens to men . . . the world's well made through."

Those who live closest to the natural world feel themselves to be an integral part of the larger web of life. Many Native American initiation rites send adolescents alone into the wilderness, where they can feel the humbling power of the forces of nature. During this vision quest, they find a personal spirit guide such as a bird, animal, or tree, through which they gain an intimate connection with the natural world. Chief Seattle says:

The perfumed flowers
are our sisters;
the deer, the horse, the great eagle,
these are our brothers.
the rocky crests,
the juices of the meadows,
the body heat of the pony, and man—
all belong to the same family.

In a similar way, the Taoists and Zen masters listen for the rhythms of the natural world and adjust themselves to those beats. Staying in touch with nature's power and mystery reminds them continually of how little they know and how small they are. Issa's haiku demonstrates the type of lessons that nature offers on how to live and die:

Simply trust—
Do not the petals flutter down,
Just like that?

Elevating human civilization above the natural world may be a fatal hubris. By walling ourselves off into cities and focusing only on the historical concerns of our species, we have cut our vital link with the rest of life. Albert Camus vividly assesses our loss in "Helen's Exile":

> What imagination could we have left for that higher
> equilibrium in which nature balanced history. . . . We
> turn our backs on nature; we are ashamed of beauty.
> Our wretched tragedies have a smell of the office
> clinging to them, and the blood that trickles from
> them is the color of printer's ink.

We are so caught up in our self-important dramas that we can't smell the poisons in the air or taste them in the water. The Western urban intellectual's long indifference to the notion of a simple, experiential understanding of the natural world may turn out to be the gravest rational error of all.

In nature we learn the vital lesson of just being. We feel the perfection of things as they are and understand what Jesus meant when he said, "Consider the lilies of the field. . . ." Perhaps our culture lacks nothing so much as a sense of this state of being. Alan Watts expressed this sentiment most eloquently in his book, *Nature, Man and Woman*.

> For what we call "nature" is free from a certain kind of
> scheming and self-importance. The birds and beasts
> indeed pursue their business of eating and breeding
> with the utmost devotion. But they do not justify it;
> they do not pretend that it serves higher ends, or that
> it makes a significant contribution to the progress of
> the world. . . . [Humanity] stands in need of . . . [a]

philosophy which, like nature, has no purpose or con-
sequence other than itself.

The crazy wisdom we gain from both art and nature is like
Zen—beyond words and concepts, without purpose or
meaning. Art and nature just are, and that is what experi-
encing them can teach.

Wonder

> *That* the world is, is the mystical.
>
> LUDWIG WITTGENSTEIN

It should be clear by now that an essential ingredient of
crazy wisdom is perspective—the understanding born of
multiple views and multiple truths. Furthermore, the spark
that keeps moving crazy wisdom from point of view to
point of view is a basic attitude of doubt. As Voltaire stated,
"Doubt is an uncomfortable condition, but certainty is a
ridiculous one."

Of course, many see doubt as a negative state, a continual restlessness or frowning skepticism. But just on the
other side of doubt lies wonder, the feeling that comes
from having an empty head and an open heart. A sense of

At the moment you are most
in awe of all there is about life
that you don't understand,
you are closer to understanding it all than at any other
time.

JANE WAGNER

wonder seems to be another key that unlocks the door to crazy wisdom and keeps it swinging open. Albert Einstein embraced the wonder that plays such a crucial role in all realms of life:

> The most beautiful experience we can have is the mysterious. It is the fundamental emotion which stands at the cradle of true art and true science. Whosoever does not know it and can no longer wonder, no longer marvel, is as good as dead, and his eyes are dimmed.

The Hindu teacher Swami Muktananda was once asked why he didn't work miracles. He replied, "I have no need to work miracles. The circulation of blood through my body is enough."

Holy fools are often awed by the world. Perhaps this comes from knowing how little they know. The mystery is simultaneously humbling and inspiring. Chuang-tzu accepts doubt and playfully wonders what might lie ahead.

> How marvelous the Creator is! What is he going to make out of you next? Where is he going to send you? Will he make you into a rat's liver? Will he make you into a bug's arm?

Religions try to capture the mystery, and put it into faces, stories, and song. Science is after the mystery too, convinced that it can be made to make sense. That science will ever solve it is doubtful, but recent scientific descriptions of reality are sliding into poetry, sounding more and more like the wonder of crazy wisdom. In his book *Fearful Symmetry,* theoretical physicist Anthony Zee makes magic out of nearly incomprehensible physical processes:

> Use the principle of local symmetry to produce grand unification, with its inevitable violation of baryon conservation. Include a little CP violation and throw in some gravity to make it all expand. And, voilá, a universe that produces its own dirt, stars, flowers, and human beings.

Perhaps the ultimate statement of crazy wisdom wonder comes from a book written in the second century B.C. in India, called *The Flower Ornament Scripture.* The mystery of existence has never been expressed in more detail than in this immense Mahayana Buddhist scripture. The book opens by using the linear, mathematical mind and then leads us beyond the limits of calculation into mythic realms. For example, in one sequence a mythical Buddha tries to explain how many worlds have come into existence. The Buddha

How wondrously super-
natural, and miraculous this!
I draw water, and I carry fuel!
P'ANG CHU-SHIH

begins calculating like this: "Ten to the tenth power times ten to the tenth power equals ten to the twentieth power. . . ." This calculating goes on for several pages. We resume near the final summation:

> . . . that squared is ten to the power of 25,373,323,152,579,663,188,831,409,602,560; that squared is ten to the power of 101,493,292,610,318,652,755,325,638,410,240; that squared is incalculable; an incalculable to the fourth power is a boundless; a boundless to the fourth power is incomparable; an incomparable to the fourth power is an innumerable; an innumerable to the fourth power is an unaccountable; an unaccountable to the fourth power is an unthinkable; an unthinkable to the fourth power is an immeasurable; an immeasurable to the fourth power is an unspeakable; an unspeakable to the fourth power is an untold, which is unspeakably unspeakable; an untold multiplied by itself is a square untold.

Then the Buddha speaks these verses:

> Untold unspeakables
> Fill all unspeakables;
> In unspeakable eons
> Explanation of the unspeakable
> cannot be finished.

If untold Buddha-lands are reduced
to atoms,
In one atom are untold lands,
And as in one,
So in each.

Working Out with the Holy Fools

Do not give rise to a single thought.

SIXTH CHINESE ZEN PATRIARCH

The holy fools want to drive us out of our minds, knowing that when we get there, the fresh air will do us good. Maybe we will begin to understand that we cannot understand and will relax a little. Only *then* will we begin to understand.

The disciple Hui-k'e asked Bodhidharma, "Please help me to quiet my mind." Bodhidharma said, "Bring me your mind so that I can quiet it." After a moment Hui-k'e said, "But I can't find my mind." "There," said Bodhidharma, "I have now quieted your mind."

CHARLES LUK

Where is the mind? Many Eastern spiritual masters do not consider the "mind" to be located in the skull. They point to the center of the chest, to the dense and complex nerve center just below the sternum, and call it the "heart-mind." Another kind of cognition or recognition may go on in this heart-mind, another way of knowing that requires a name other than knowledge. Using the hyphen, as above, we can refer to it as "being-knowledge."

According to Eastern holy fools, the continual buzz in the mind—of facts and figurings, desires and regrets, plans and fantasies—prevents us from finding crazy wisdom. Our minds are so full of words that there is no room for wisdom, our psyches so busy working that being-knowledge stays far away.

Go ahead. Get your mind to stop and allow you a glimpse into just being. Experience this moment without qualifying or thinking about it. You might begin by trying to go for two or three minutes without any thoughts at all. Most people find it very difficult to halt the constant pulse of messages. This kind of experiment is a hint that we are not in charge of our own mental life. A more intensive and thorough investigation of ourselves reveals the shocking extent to which our thoughts and feelings are not under the direction of any free will or independent self.

Eastern holy fools, who sometimes refer to the mind as "the wild monkey," have invented many exercises to tame it. They created meditation techniques that allowed them to study themselves and become free from mental and emotional conditioning.

The West has tended to rely on observational rather than experiential studies of the human condition. We focus our microscopes on cells and subatomic particles, observe rats and chimpanzees and extrapolate to our own situation, or set up experiments in which one group of humans studies another. These methods lead us to what could be called *informative* knowledge, but not *transformative* knowledge—not wisdom. The spiritual teacher Ram Dass describes the difference this way:

> You can either be wise or you can know knowledge. But you can't know wisdom, you have to "be" it. Wisdom has simplicity to it. What the spiritual path offers is a way to come back into balance, to develop our intuition and the wisdom of our heart, so that the intellect is no longer the master, but instead is the servant of our heart . . . the part of us that brings us into unity with ourselves and all other beings.

The mad mind does not halt. If it halts, it is enlightenment.
CHINESE ZEN SAYING

By definition, human beings do not see or hear. I broke loose from definition.
RUMI

The practice of mediation involves an intuitive, experiential mode of perception that has nothing to do with reason or knowledge. Meditation seems to activate a special psychic process, only recently acknowledged and explored by Western science. In *The Psychology of Consciousness,* Robert Ornstein speculates about the effects of meditation:

> The "mystic" experience brought about by concentrative meditation, and other techniques is . . . a shift from the normal, analytic world containing separate, discrete objects and persons to a second mode, an experience of "unity" and holistic perception . . . it is a complementary dimension of consciousness that adds to and can give comprehension to the ordered sequence of "normal" thought.

Meditation techniques include the mantra (repeating of phrases or patterns of syllables), visualization (holding images steady in the mind), and concentration on a single object or action, such as one's breath. These practices develop strength and focus of mind, enabling meditators to see through their individual obsessions and confusion to discover what is often referred to as our true nature. Poet

When you try to understand everything, you will not understand anything. The best way is to understand yourself, and then you will understand everything.

SHUNRYU SUZUKI

Gary Snyder's Zen training led him to understand the process this way:

> Wisdom is intuitive knowledge of the mind of love and clarity that lies beneath one's ego-driven anxieties and aggressions. Meditation is going into the mind to see this for yourself—over and over again, until it becomes the mind you live in.

Eastern holy fools say that, fundamentally, meditation is a practice of being. Although this sounds contradictory, it seems that humans do have to *practice* being in order to do it properly. We habitually try to analyze and adjust our environment, as though it were never quite right or as if we were in constant danger. Meditation practice is an antidote to our desires and fears, a way to allow ourselves to be in the world as it is.

Getting beyond the self is one of the most important results of meditation practice. Once we see the reactive, conditioned nature of our thoughts and emotions, we begin to lose our attachment to them; we no longer identify so strongly with our personality. Understanding our lack of freedom also gives us empathy for the common predicament of all human beings. From these insights can come a feeling

When you set yourself free from life and death, you should know your ultimate destination. So when the four elements separate, where will you go?

KOAN, MASTER TOSOTSU ETSU

What was my fundamental face before I was born?

ZEN KOAN

If knowledge does not liberate the self from the self, then ignorance is better than such knowledge.

HAKIM SINAI

of unity, as well as the great love and compassion that so often guide the holy fools in their responses to the world. Once the wild monkey mind has been tamed, it can become the servant of the heart, "a mind of love and clarity." When there is no "you," it is all you.

> To become a spectator of one's own life is to escape the suffering of life.
>
> OSCAR WILDE

Meditation might be considered theater. Think of it as a ticket to step outside yourself in order to get some distance on your own little drama—to become not only an actor on the world's stage but a member of the audience as well. This process helps us understand our personas as the masks that they are—the archetypes we are cast to portray. As part of the audience we can view the production we are in as "a play"—sometimes a parody, and at times a musical comedy. To some, it may all look like the theater of the absurd.

The theater of meditation requires that part of the mind be trained as an observer, known as the witness, the other, or the higher self. Climb into the balcony of your consciousness and find a seat. Once you see yourself from up there, everything takes a different look. This point of reference is sometimes called getting a cosmic perspective.

If you are going to practice this theater game, crazy wisdom has some advice: Give your observer a sense of humor. No need to have a grim higher self. Just put a wry, bemused smile on the face of your witness. Your *cosmic* perspective can also be a *comic* perspective. If we just get some distance, the cosmic and comic become One and the same. And the joke is on us all.

> We are not free. And the sky can still fall on our heads. And the theater has been created to teach us that first of all.
>
> ANTONIN ARTAUD

CHAPTER 8

Crazy Wisdom on the Road

We will now try our own exercises in crazy wisdom. Borrowing methods from Socrates and Chuang-tzu, we will turn over a few persistent and puzzling questions that we humans ask about ourselves and the universe. This exercise should loosen our attitude and beliefs, and allow our minds to stretch. Think of it as a crazy wisdom workout.

For our exercise in crazy wisdom we will call on the help of some of the crazy wisdom characters we met earlier. With Coyote in the lead, a Taoist sage on our right, and the Jester on our left, followed by a few Zen masters and a pack of clowns, artists, philosophers, and scientists, we now take up our poetry books and walking staffs and begin a journey through the mind of the world, tracking the river of questions to the foot of the tall mountain of answers. Once there we will climb and explore, look under rocks and behind theories, inside DNA molecules and spinning subatomic particles, and gaze out over vast vistas of space-time to consider the perennial puzzles of the universe.

The scientists are very important to our journey, as they will provide the most recent "facts" and theories about everything. To ensure both a micro and macro perspective—a physicist who sees "in depth" and an astronomer who sees "far out." We will also bring along a biologist, a psychologist, an anthropologist, a geologist, and assorted other "ologists"—the truth holders of the current culture. The Jester suggests that what we really need is a generalist, an astro-physio-bio-psycho-anthro-geo-paleontologist, to synthesize it all. That way, we could save on supplies and overhead. Unfortunately, no such being exists.

Where do we start? Let us imagine that one of our Zen masters, realizing that the first step is arbitrary, simply begins chanting, "Who? Who? Who?" Our journey begins with the most elementary enigma.

Who Do You Think You Are?

Be humble for you are made of dung. Be noble for you are made of the stars.

SERBIAN PROVERB

In the beginning—about fifteen billion years ago according to the latest scientific evidence, give or take a few billion years—there was a big bang: the great cosmic orgasm. Out of that first fireball came the spin of atoms and the pattern of molecules, the cooked and cooling contents of the cosmic

Perhaps whales came into being because nature had a lot of extra plankton and squid. What evolutionary vacuum sucked humans into existence?

GARY SNYDER

soup, blasting away from itself in all directions with a force that still reverberates in exploding stars and in our voices. And we still are "big bangin'" away.

Only 3,500 million years ago, give or take a few million years, a bolt of lightning struck the oozing primal mud with such force and finesse that it turned chemistry into biology. The combination of electricity and chemicals started off the multiple mutations that became us, the strange species of protoplasm we call human, conscious of ourselves and aware that we will die, spinning through space on this lukewarm blue-green sphere without knowing for sure why we are here or what we are supposed to be doing.

Who are we and how do we fit into the bigger picture? And why do we place such grave importance on our lives and the life of our species? Has some poorly built survival mechanism made us into such awkward egocentrics and human chauvinists? Looking back on the long difficult road of biological evolution, covering three and a half billion years, what makes us believe we are its final destination?

Let's take a close look at ourselves, individually, standing alone and naked. You go first. (We call in a physicist and a biochemist for this examination.) Let's see now—looking closely we find that your body is made up of approximately 80 percent water. (The Jester calls the body "the sublime slime.") As we investigate further, we find that this water, along with everything else in your body, is made entirely of atoms; looking even closer we find that those atoms are almost entirely empty space. Now, if your body is made of atoms, and atoms are just empty space, then what is holding your clothes on? Not only does the emperor have no clothes . . . the clothes have no emperor! Maybe all of us are just illusions in somebody's magic act.

At this point, a Zen master bops us with his staff, and we have to conclude that human beings are at least real enough to feel pain. It is even possible that we are the most important reality of all. We know we want to be. What other creature can remove a piece of tree and make chopsticks from it? Which other species buys insurance? Possessing the power to think abstractly and the power to manipulate objects has led us to believe, perhaps rightly, that as individuals and as a species, we do have a special place in creation.

Nonetheless, there have always been humans among us who believe that we are not all that special, and not even very smart. A few skeptical jesters have had the audacity to make a case against their own species, denying that we are the perfect molecular mixture, the cellular summit.

> If man had created man he would be ashamed of his performance.
>
> MARK TWAIN

They refuse to have such a low opinion of nature as to believe that humans are the best it can do. In *A Mencken Chrestomathy,* the jester H. L. Mencken takes a clear-eyed look at our species' physical attributes.

> All the errors and incompetencies of the Creator reach their climax in man. As a piece of mechanism he is the worst of them all; put beside him, even a salmon or a staphylococcus is a sound and efficient machine. He has the worst kidneys known to comparative zoology, and the worst lungs, and the worst heart. His eye, considering the work it is called upon to do, is less efficient than the eye of an earthworm; an optical instrument maker who made an instrument so clumsy would be mobbed by his customers. Alone of all the animals, terrestrial, celestial or marine, man is unfit by nature to go abroad in the world he inhabits. He must clothe himself, protect himself, swathe himself, armor himself. He is eternally in the position of a turtle born without a shell, a dog without hair, a fish without fins. Lacking his heavy and cumbersome trappings, he is defenseless even against flies. As God made him he hasn't even a tail to switch them off.

Mark Twain also held the opinion that we are an incompetently built species. In "Satan's Letter from the Earth," he makes it clear that our limitations are not only physical:

> [Man] . . . is constantly inflicted with a defect . . . the
> Moral Sense. It is the secret of his degradation. It is
> the quality which enables him to do wrong. Without
> it, man could do no wrong. He would rise at once to
> the level of the Higher Animals.

Twain saw the human species as disjointed, out of harmony
with itself and the rest of creation. His opinion of "The
Damned Human Race" was that we are on the bottom
rung of evolution's ladder.

> . . . we have descended and degenerated, from some
> far ancestor—some microscopic atom wandering at
> its pleasure between the mighty horizons of a drop of
> water perchance—insect by insect, animal by animal,
> reptile by reptile, down the long highways of smirch-
> less innocence, till we have reached the bottom stage
> of development—nameable as the Human Being.
> Below us—nothing. Nothing but the Frenchman.

Quite a few psychologists (as well as some holy fools) have
added their voices to Mencken's and Twain's, reminding us
that for the most part we are "unconscious," barely aware
of or in control of ourselves, often ruled by much the same
forces as these beings we call "the lower animals." (Coyote

> Nature has no instructions
> for mankind except that our
> poor beleaguered humanist-
> democratic way of life, our
> fantasies of the individual's
> high worth, our sense that
> the weak, no less than the
> strong, have a right to survive,
> are absurd.
>
> JOYCE CAROL OATES

looks up from what he is doing and winks.) And one more thing. Even if human beings are at the top of the evolutionary ladder, we sure did step on a lot of toes getting here—passenger pigeon toes and the three toes of the three-toed sloth, to name just a few. Since the story isn't over yet, we might well ask who or what will step on human toes on their climb to the top.

In the last two centuries we have switched the focus of our investigation of who we are from the creation story to the evolutionary sciences. We no longer ask what God is like, or why He made us the way we are, and instead we try to figure out how molecules and cells transformed themselves into consciousness and the opposable thumb. The tentative conclusions we have come up with are somewhat surprising.

For instance, fossil records show that approximately one million years ago, the human brain suddenly began to grow at an unprecedented rate, adding about one cubic inch every hundred thousand years. Then the growth rate doubled, and doubled again, until the brain was growing by ten cubic inches every hundred thousand years. Some scientists speculate that the phenomenal growth was fueled by a great ice age, the first in a few million years, and thus the first since human inhabited the planet. By the time the glaciers were advancing, about eight hundred thousand years ago, humans had already migrated to northern regions of the earth from their point of origin near the equator and the drastic climate change required man to develop new survival skills. Some scientists speculate that the brain's sudden growth was stimulated by those ice age requirements.

In other words it may be nothing but ice that started the fire in our skulls. Our great energy and ingenuity could simply be the result of being cold; consciousness may be nature's way of shoveling snow! What, then, can we make of the elaborate civilizations and cultures that evolved during the last few hundred thousand years? Perhaps they are side effects of nervous energy left over from our struggle to conquer the elements—energy that continues to find outlets in nuclear bombs and symphonies and skyscrapers full of people writing coded message to each other. Perhaps war itself is a response left over from a time of competition for scarce resources, a time dominated by our fear of the cold. All that we do today may be the final shivers of an age, not so long ago, when we did not have central heating.

Our most recent scientific discoveries raise doubts about our lofty place in the cosmic scheme. Are we the Creator's pets or just another complex chemical compound?

We are a tiny little twig of the mammalian tree, an after-thought. Nature was not made for us.

STEPHEN JAY GOULD

Is consciousness uniquely human, or is there consciousness everywhere; and if so, did we get the wrong dose? Are we stuck in a transitional time warp, our lives merely a phase like the one between fish and frog, crawling from sea to land in an evolutionary midlife crisis? Must we go back to our webbed feet to navigate the landscape after the oceans rise? What part of our anatomy will begin to grow and lead us to our next destiny? What sleek new species is waiting to be born from our dilemmas? And meanwhile, what genetic backwater has left us washed up on the shore of this age, gasping for breath, caught between what we were and what we will yet become? Who or what could have designed us like this, floundering between feelings of self-importance and doubt? In the big story of life, who could we be? Scientist Robert Ardery offers this guess:

We are the missing link.

We need to pause here for the moment. It seems an argument has broken out between a few members of our wandering troupe. Some philosophers and scientists are quarreling over whether we can ever know who we are. A clown, hearing this dispute, tries to solve the problem by simply introducing

people to each other. A Zen master is impressed by this solu-
tion and bows to the clown. The Zen master then asks, "Isn't
it also true that we are what we eat?" On hearing this, the
Jester rolls his eyes and says, "If you are what you eat, then
why be a vegetable? Why not eat people who are smarter
and better looking than you?" Surprisingly, the Jester does
not get hit with a staff for this remark.

In the hope that greater perspective might give us
some answers, an astronomer suggests that we head out
into space to look at humans from there. We know that
the farther away we get from ourselves, the smaller we will
look. The Jester adds, "And, the better we will look."

Of course, to live on a planet is to live in outer space
already. Once we get off the earth we are able to see that
clearly. In fact, one of the best views of earth is from
space. Once we get far enough away, we won't see dead
animals on the roadsides or beer cans in the rivers or the
grimacing faces of city commuters. If we get far enough
away, the earth doesn't look dirty. It doesn't even look
"earthy." It looks more like a misted marble or slightly
sucked-on, dampish blue gumball.

If we had been monitoring earth from our perch
here in space during the past few hundred million years,

we might have detected an ominous new development. Up until about one hundred years ago the earth seemed relatively stable. Of course glaciers and continents slowly shifted and the occasional volcano erupted, but nothing too dramatic. The earth was just another cooling hunk of stuff. Then suddenly, at the beginning of the twentieth century, a series of atmospheric disturbances occurred: Waves began radiating from the earth—electrical waves, sound waves, light waves—leaping into the sky and out into space. Some waves had definite patterns, and anyone on another planet able to detect these patterns might have surmised that intelligent life was transmitting messages. To creatures who could not detect the patterns, it may have looked as if the earth had started decaying.

Also about a hundred years ago, big hunks of solid matter began leaving the earth's surface. Objects in the shapes of large birds flew out and back again. Out and back. As time went on, more and more, and bigger and bigger objects came off, and soon, big cylinders shot off the planet and orbited around it. In a very short period, the space surrounding the earth, previously empty, became filled with pieces of the earth itself. From anywhere else in space, our planet must have looked as if it had started coming apart.

Could it be that technology is an unwitting euphemism for the process of entropy? Are we simply agents of this planet's disintegration, catalysts for an evolutionary process that takes place without our knowledge or choice?

As we look around the universe, we realize that the big bang set enormous forces into motion and created huge galaxies of burning stars, each locked into some inexorable course. We see that we are part of this celestial movement and completely at its mercy. If the universe keeps expanding, eventually thinning into nothing, we will go with it. If the universe collapses back on itself (in what scientists call the big crunch) and another big bang starts a new cycle, then we may be reborn, too, in one form or another.

The physicists in our group agree that we are intimately connected to the cosmos, but they look at it from another point of view. Deep inside matter, they are finding that each subatomic event is affected by all other subatomic events everywhere in space-time, even when separated by great distances. To describe this interdependence, physicists claim that reality is "non-local," meaning that the entire universe and everything that happens within it is one interconnected web of occurrence. No autonomy and no separate purpose can exist.

Life is a disease of matter.
GERALD FINEBERG

We are, ultimately, the product of primeval forces mediated by the X and Y bosons.

ANTHONY ZEE

The Taoist sage reminds us that being part of every-thing does not make us less, it makes us more. Gesturing all around us, he quotes the Hindus, who are fond of saying, "Thou art That." Meanwhile, the Jester—a little bored out here in space with no civilization to poke fun at—wants us to move closer to earth. The clowns feel right at home flying around with the furniture in this weightless environment, but a vote is taken and we head back toward home.

As we approach earth from our perch in space, we start to get a better view of all the little creatures that live and die on the surface of the planet. Looking at things from a closer distance we find that, contrary to what we often assume, humans are not masters of the other forms of life on earth. In *Timescale,* Nigel Calder speculates that plants are earth's real rulers.

> . . . certain cunning plants have taken over the choicest parts of the Earth's surface . . . their apparent passivity is deceptive: they manipulate the animals. [These plants] . . . have recruited battalions of small six-legged and large two-legged animals to serve them. The reproductive self-interest of the plants requires that animals find their flowers attractive, their nectar and fruit tasty. Beside a bed of particularly elegant flowers, a biped stoops in a humble posture, carefully removing any

plants except those that have charmed him to their
service. Other bipeds swarm in large numbers around
the green rectangles in the river valleys.

The master of the planet is now identifiable: it is
grass. Grass first evolved its biped slaves, the human
beings, as hunters on the grasslands, and then lured
them into the cultivation of special grasses, including wheat, rice, and maize. With unstinted effort, the
humans cleared trees and other plants out of the way,
and they irrigated the kempt fields for the benefit
of grass.

Even if the amber waves of grain are not in charge, we are
totally dependent on them, and should perhaps honor and
pray to the goddesses of grasses more than we have. Maybe
we aren't giving due attention to the grasses because we
have switched our allegiance to a different master. In *Auto-
geddon*, Heathcote Williams writes:

> If an alien were to hover a few
> hundred yards above the planet
> It could be forgiven for thinking
> That cars were the dominant life-form,
> And that human beings were a kind of
> ambulatory fuel cell:
> Injected when the car wished to move off,
> And ejected when they were spent.

Are automobiles our new master, intentionally destroying the grasses as they take over the human slave market? Grasses or automobiles, or all manner of material goods—in the final analysis, as Ralph Waldo Emerson saw, "things are in the saddle and ride mankind."

As our group settles back down to earth and feels the pull of gravity again, we really start wondering where our freedom lies. Although most of us admit we are not in charge of the matter and energy of the cosmos or the life of our planet, we still feel we are in control of our own destinies—at least in little ways. A few artists and philosophers in our group insist they are free and independent, and furthermore, that they are significant (famous, even immortal) in the larger scheme of things. To answer them, the Taoist master faces the wind, letting his long beard and hair be whipped about by the invisible element, and audibly breaks a little wind himself. With a slight sentimental shrug, he says, "Our greatest bondage may be to the illusion that we are free."

Freedom's Just Another Word

The perceptual blind spot that gives us the impression that we are separate from the rest of creation may have also fostered the belief that we are in control, not only of our environment but also of ourselves. Debate over the truth of this belief used to be primarily a religious matter, and centered on the amount of freedom the Creator had given us to act, or more specifically, to sin or not to sin. Back when most of Western civilization believed that God was in control of our lives, we assumed that He could be bribed with a few good deeds or contrite supplications, which left us some degree of choice over our destiny. However, in the modern era, science has investigated the free will/determinism question by taking a close look at the biological and psychological makeup of the individual. And, as the ancient saying goes, self-knowledge is usually bad news.

> Do you think I know what I'm doing?
> That for one breath or half-breath I belong to myself?
> As much as a pen knows what it's writing,
> Or the ball can guess where it's going next.
>
> RUMI

What science is discovering about the human condition conforms with much of what holy fools have understood for centuries. It seems to come down to this: Not only are we not in charge of the cosmos or the planet, we are barely in charge of ourselves. This has serious implications for the Western worldview, something Freud realized early in the twentieth century:

> Humanity has in the course of time had to endure from the hands of science two great outrages upon its self-love. The first was when it realized that our earth was not the center of the universe . . . . The second was when biological research robbed man of his peculiar privilege of having been specially created, and relegated him to descent from the animal world, implying an irradicable animal nature in him . . . . But man's craving for grandiosity is now suffering the third and most bitter blow from present day psychological research, which is endeavoring to prove to the ego in each one of us that he is not even master in his own house . . . .

We may never know the extent to which we are free, but it seems safe to say that we attribute to ourselves much more freedom than we actually have. Most people feel they act independently from moment to moment; few even consider the question, since we have absorbed the assumption of free will so thoroughly. While some acknowledge the influence of past biological and psychological conditioning, it is usually not an internalized awareness, and we forget, when involved in life from moment to moment, the truth of the matter.

Human freedom seems to be severely circumscribed by our fundamental biochemical makeup. Science writer Jon Franklin studied the field of molecular psychology and, in his Pulitzer Prize–winning book, *Molecules of the Mind*, asserts that our belief in free will is itself determined:

> And so, multileveled Mother Nature, wry and cruel but at times strangely benevolent, has inserted a mechanism in the mechanism to prevent that mechanism from fully comprehending its mechanistic nature. Faith itself, in other words, is but a mechanism.

Biochemists are reporting that moods and emotions are closely associated with certain chemicals. What we call love, for example, may be understood as the presence of an "excitant amine" known as phenylethylamine, or PEA, in our system. Mice injected with PEA jump up and down and vocalize, while rhesus monkeys exhibit "lip smacking behavior."(Coyote wants to know where he can buy some of this stuff.)

Meanwhile, the latest evidence indicates that each of us is shackled from birth to a genetically determined future, bound by the chains of the DNA double helix. Biogeneticists tell us that the DNA molecule is programmed with information that determines how tall we will grow and how strong our teeth will be, what illnesses we are likely to contract, and to some degree, how long we will live. It is as if we are each born into a mystery novel, and as the plot unfolds, our identity is gradually revealed. Our genes provide each of us with a face that we must wear from birth to death, unless, we can afford a new one. A thick head of hair or a nearsighted squint or lopsided ears—we each are given features that affect how the world looks at us, and therefore how we look back at the world. (The clowns glance at each other and start to laugh.) On the physical level, at least, we are not free to be ourselves; we are forced to be ourselves. Each of us is imprisoned in our cells.

Our belief in individual autonomy is also seriously challenged by recent brain research, which reveals that humans actually have three brains, sometimes referred to as the reptilian brain, mammalian brain, and the new cerebral

Did you know the RNA/DNA molecule can be found throughout space in many galaxies . . . only everybody spells it differently.

JANE WAGNER

cortex, or "human" brain. These brains are wired closely together, and scientists believe that much of our behavior emerges from the evolutionary programming of the two pre-human brains. Some even suggest that we use our new human brain primarily to justify the actions generated by the two older brains. In other words, much of our thinking is just a way to make excuses for ourselves as we go along. (Coyote winks again.)

In *Galapagos,* Kurt Vonnegut looks back at our world from a million years in the future, by which time it is obvious that today's brains did not work very well:

> Apologies for momentary brain failures were the staple of everybody's conversations: "Whoops," "Excuse me," "I hope you're not hurt," "I can't believe I did that," "It happened so fast I didn't have time to think," "I have insurance against this kind of thing," and "How can I ever forgive myself?," and "I didn't know it was loaded," and on and on.

Someday the brain's evolution may provide us with a more comprehensive or different type of self-awareness, which will allow us the freedom to act instead of just reacting. We may need to become more conscious before we can be free. As the poet Robert Bly states:

Contemplating the mechanism of our own minds and gazing morosely on the chemical action and reaction that equate with consciousness and personality, we seem directed toward the dark conclusion that free will is but a concept designed, like Santa Claus or God, to shield us from the unacceptable truth. The truth, we are terrified of learning, is that we are chaff in the wind . . . .

JON FRANKLIN

> The reptile brain has embodied itself in the outer world in the form of a tank which even moves like a reptile. A "saint" is someone who has managed to move away from the reptile and the mammal brains and is living primarily in the new brain.

From another angle, psychologists tell us that individual freedom is completely circumscribed by our early upbringing. As infants, we ingest our parents and then spend the rest of our lives trying to digest them. We eat them whole, from their genes to their judgments. We eat their values, their fears, their moods, their worldviews; even if we rebel against them, they shape that rebellion. Their voices continuously echo inside of us. We never leave home.

Psychologists tell us that we are stuck inside personalities that are almost completely formed in our earliest years, long before we could decide who we wanted to be. Considering humanity's lofty view of itself, we might find Freudian theory especially humbling—much of who we are depends on how we were potty trained.

Meanwhile, volumes have been written about how we are programmed to conform to the values and fashions of the society into which we are born. Adding another dimension, geological anthropologists (or anthropological

A person is never himself, but always a mask; a person never owns his own person, but always represents another, by whom he is possessed. And the other that one is, is always ancestors . . . .

NORMAN O. BROWN

geologists) talk about "geographic determinism"—the
hypothesis that our perception of reality is shaped, at least
partially, by the mountains or the flatlands that surround us.

Cosmic, geological, biological, psychological, cultural,
political—so many forces shape us. And we haven't even
mentioned the possibility of past lives influencing the present one. Can we make a case for some degree of individual
autonomy or personal freedom? Our Taoist sage offers a
paradoxical answer from Chuang-tzu, his favorite source:

> Let your mind wander in simplicity, blend your spirit
> with the vastness, follow along with things the way
> they are, and make no room for personal views—then
> the world will be governed.

Most members of our group are intrigued with this question of human freedom. A few clowns stick out their
tongues and bop each other, trying to prove they are free
by acting spontaneously, until a philosopher points out
that this is their normal behavior, and thus predictable. In
the melee, a Zen master gets bopped by mistake; he claims
that he demonstrates his freedom by choosing not to react
to the blow. He gets bopped again, this time intentionally.
Meanwhile, an artist who is hungry for new scenery points

out that we are going around in circles and getting nowhere. The Taoist sage remarks, "We are getting nowhere only because we think we are going somewhere in the first place." Hearing this, a clown asks innocently, "Well if we aren't going somewhere, then why are we here?" At this, everyone bursts into laughter.

> Life is too important a thing ever to talk seriously about it.
>
> OSCAR WILDE

Why Are We Here?

> The meaning of life is that it stops.
>
> FRANZ KAFKA

Contemporary street wisdom informs us that "Life's a bitch and then you die." This could be the first line of a couplet ending with the line: "And nobody knows the reason why." What is the meaning of this life we live?

Existential uncertainty is difficult if not impossible for many people to live with. Knowledge is our survival mechanism, and we have a nervous biological craving to know what is going on here. We want certainty, especially about the meaning of our lives, and if we can't find certainty in knowledge, then many will turn to blind faith. In *Waiting for Godot,* Samuel Beckett suggests that blind is the only kind of faith there is.

> VLADIMIR: What are we doing here, that is the question. And we are blessed in this, that we happen to know the answer. Yes, in this immense confusion one thing alone is clear. We are waiting for Godot to come . . . .

We can't accept that life is nothing more than the moments between birth and death. That would be absurd! Our existence—our suffering—must have some greater significance, and if the universe won't tell us what it is, then we will have to make something up. Enter the multitude of gods and religions. (Choose one of the above.)

In this secular era, many old gods have been replaced with ideologies, or "isms," or nation-states, or even life-styles. If we can't discover the one supreme reason for existing, we create relatively satisfying earthbound purposes: a utopian future, or "freedom," or "progress," or "the children," or "all the gusto." We also have Joseph Campbell's view:

The believer is happy, the doubter is wise.
GREEK PROVERB

> I don't believe life has a purpose. Life is a lot of proto-
> plasm with an urge to reproduce and continue in being.

Maybe that's all we're here to do: "Go forth and multiply."
Just be and beget and be and beget and be and beget, until
some cosmic catastrophe ends it all. Or maybe one great
truth or purpose does exist for which all of us are living or
should be living, and we just don't know it yet. One day
we may discover we were put here to serve as hosts for
microbes that are the Creator's true chosen ones. Or
maybe we are part of someone's experiment to determine
whether we can figure out why we are here, and our confusion, like that of rats in a maze, is the whole point.

Perhaps someday the one true god or goddess will
appear and say, "Nobody got my name right." Or maybe
all deities exist but none of them are "good," and they
take no interest in whether or not we are good. Could it be
that all these years we have been good only for goodness'
sake? Maybe all of our questions will be answered one
day. Maybe they won't. Gertrude Stein claims she has
found the answer:

> There ain't no answer.
> There ain't going to be any answer.
> There never has been an answer.
> That's the answer.

But this raises another question. If we aren't meant to know, then why this "why?" Another damn "why!" Why why why? What kind of joke is this? Why do we carry the "why" chromosome? Where will our questions lead us?

> God made man because he loves stories.
> YIDDISH SAYING

Let's assume that we are here to provide stories. Here is a good one. Once upon a time, in fact only a few hundred years ago, most Westerners believed that humans lived on a planet that was located at the very center of the universe. Then a great scientist named Galileo figured out that the earth circles the sun, and therefore the sun must be the center. The Catholic church, believing that humans had been specially created and therefore that the earth had to be the center of the universe, forced Galileo to recant. This took place back in the 1630s, but the Church did not officially forgive Galileo until 1979. By then, astronomers and physicists had discovered that the sun itself is a relatively small star located in the edge of a relatively small galaxy in a cosmos that includes billions of galaxies filled with uncountable billions of stars. The Vatican absolved Galileo, but made no further pronouncement as to the center of the universe.

So where is the center of the universe? And where are we in relation to it? Have we been pushed into the wings? Is earth just a backdrop for a truly meaningful drama happening thousands of galaxies away, and humanity merely a crowd of extras spinning around the lead characters who play their parts on center stage—light-years from earth?

Like any crazy wisdom story, this one has yet another twist. Astronomers figure that the big bang sent everything in the universe moving away from everything else uniformly in all directions, so that, in fact, every single point in the universe can be considered the center. "That's you, baby!" the Jester says, laughing. "You are still the center of the universe, just as you always believed and hoped you were!"

The clowns puff out their chests, obviously proud, but a physicist stands up and clears his throat to get their attention. Holding up a picture of Albert Einstein for effect, he reminds us that it is impossible to locate ourselves in space (where we are) unless we simultaneously locate our-selves in time (when we are). Where and when are one. This may mean that, as many of us have suspected, maps and clocks are unreliable.

Our group agrees that the time has come to look at time. But first, we must synchronize ourselves in the moment. The Zen master shouts, "Be here now!" After looking around, he concludes that everyone missed that particular moment. "Don't worry," he says, "the here and now will come around again. Next time, be prepared."

Time Out

> Read not the Times, read the Eternities.
>
> HENRY DAVID THOREAU

One way crazy wisdom gets crazy and wise is by playing with time—going into the past or the future to see what the present looks like from a different angle. Travel broadens. Time travel changes everything.

Humans today divide their lifespans and their history into segments: millennia, centuries, decades, years, months, hours, minutes, seconds. People need to know when rent is

There was a young lady
  named Bright
Whose speed was much
  faster than light.
She went out one day
  In a relative way,
And returned the previous
  night.

ANONYMOUS

due, how long the egg has been boiling, and whether they are wearing the appropriate costume for this decade. However, the popular saying "Your time is what you make of it" may be true in more ways than one. Whether your life is long or short depends entirely on your expectations and your concept of time.

For example, scientists keep finding evidence that indicates the universe is older than previously thought, and our own lifetimes seem to shrink in comparison. On the other hand, we still live a long time compared to the mayfly, whose life lasts only a day. What if the weather is bad on that particular day? A mayfly's whole life could be rained out. Even within our own species, there is great variation. Consider that, compared to people in the East, people in the Western world measure time and history almost as though they were mayflies.

The Time of Your Lives

The world was created on the 22nd October, 4004 B.C. at 6 o'clock in the evening.

JAMES USHER
Archbishop of Armagh, 1581–1656

[Heaven and earth] and man was created by the
Trinity on the 23rd of October 4004 B.C. at 9 o'clock
in the morning.

DR. JOHN LIGHTFOOT
Vice Chancellor of the University of Cambridge, in 1859,
correcting by 15 hours Bishop Usher's estimate of two
centuries earlier

Western belief systems have stuck us firmly in the limited
spectrum of recorded human history, with very little
breathing room. The Judeo-Christian tradition claims that
the universe is just a few thousand years old, which does
not give life much of a past, and leaves no room for the
dinosaurs.

Judeo-Christian history lends current human affairs
significance far beyond that allowed by the vast timetables
of other cultures. The eternal cycles found in Asian and
Native American mythology are absent from Western
belief. We are told that Jehovah made the world in a week,
that earth is the only world there has ever been or ever will
be, and that human history is the primary measure of time.

Eastern cosmologies include endless cycles, and worlds
upon worlds. In the Hindu cosmology, one universe or
"world system" is equivalent to just one day in the life of

their supreme deity, Brahma. One hundred years of these "days," or 311,000 billion human years, completes the supreme deity's lifespan. However, according to the Hindu text, the Brahmavaivarta Purana, not even Brahma, the creator, can lord it over time: "Brahma follows Brahma; one sinks, the next arises; the endless series cannot be told."

Buddhist cosmology describes a granite mountain seven miles high and seven miles wide, and every one hundred years a crow with a silk scarf in its beak flies over the mountain, brushing the top of the peak. The time it takes for that scarf to wear down the granite mountain makes up one world cycle. Then, of course, another granite mountain appears. Make room for the crow, Sisyphus.

Anthropologist-philosopher Mircea Eliade claims that these Eastern concepts of time result in a "metaphysical depreciation of human history." In the vastness of "incalculable" universes, how important can we be?

With the big bang theory, which places the age of the universe at about fifteen billion years, Western science is just beginning to peek into the vastness of time. Astrophysicists are now hypothesizing the big crunch, during which our universe will collapse into a single particle and then, possibly, explode in another big bang. When the

Dalai Lama, the Tibetan Buddhist leader, was asked what he thought of the big bang theory, he replied, laughing, "Oh yes, we know about that. But it's not just one Bang. It's Bang, Bang, Bang!" It could be that the West is finally coming into its own version of the ancient Eastern worldview: the cyclical, repeating nature of time and universes. The difference is that our understanding of these cycles will be through the language of black holes and curved space, rather than through visions of granite mountains or of Lord Shiva, who creates and destroys world systems with each step of his dancing feet.

Our crazy wisdom group is resting. Coyote begins howling at the moon, but we can't be sure which of the infinity of moons he howls at, or what world system it belongs to. Meanwhile, a few astrophysicists are feverishly trying to figure out if Asian cosmology could fit into their current theories. Our scientists are concerned that if space and time are truly "incalculable," then a lot of mathematicians will be out of jobs and a considerable number of Nobel Prizes may have to be returned.

One puzzled astrophysicist asks the Taoist how those ancient Eastern sages came to their understanding of time and world cycles without infrared tracking devices and radio telescopes. The Taoist answers enigmatically, "By paying attention." At this point, the Zen master interjects, "The only instrument that tells time accurately is the stomach. When we get hungry, it's time to eat; beyond that, all this talk makes little difference." The Jester, who is beginning to like these Zen sayings, jumps up and raises his hand to give the Zen master a high five, but the Zen master hits him with his staff instead and shouts, "It makes a big difference!"

Oriental and Occidental ideas of time create distinctly different attitudes toward life. The Judeo-Christian worldview, with its single universe, gives each of us just this one lifetime, and in the end, God will judge how well we performed. The verdict will determine whether we spend eternity in heaven or hell. What a heavy burden! One or two mistakes and we are doomed forever, unless of course we are one of God's chosen, who will be forgiven for all sins. Pray that you pray to the right deity!

In the West, even those who don't actively believe in the Judeo-Christian mythology are deeply influenced by it. Most of us live as though this lifetime were the final exam, the first and last chance. In the West we hear, "You only go around once in life so reach for all the gusto." The Truth in

Advertising Council should have required the beer manu-
facturer who used that slogan to prove that we only go
around once. A great percentage of the world's population
doesn't believe it.

Both the Hindu and Buddhist views of life are much
more open-ended. In these belief systems, humans are given
many lifetimes to achieve perfection and salvation. In fact,
in Hinduism everyone is destined to rebirth after rebirth
until each person finally has the experience of *moksha,* or
enlightenment, and can leave the rebirth wheel. In other
words, in the Hindu system, we are all saved eventually. If
you are tired of the go-round and want to get off sooner,
you work harder, but everyone and everything makes it
someday. Making it means that you return to the uncre-
ated, unconditioned state—the uncarved block, the void,
the blankness of perfect peaceful nothing.

But wait! The Eastern cosmology with its multiple
lifetimes and eventual salvation is not all good news.
According to Eliade, a philosophy that believes in rebirth:

> . . . terrorizes man and compels him to realize that he
> must begin this same evanescent existence over and
> over again, billions of times, always enduring the

> same endless sufferings. And the effect of this is to exacerbate his will to escape, to impel him to transcend his condition as an "existent" once and for all.

The Buddha said that the tears one individual sheds throughout a cycle of lifetimes could fill all the rivers, lakes, and oceans on earth. For people who believe in reincarnation, the idea of many more lifetimes looms over them as an appalling proposition, perhaps somewhat akin to the Western concept of an eternity in purgatory. East or West, take your pick. If it isn't one thing, it's another.

According to most Eastern mythologies, we can be reborn in different forms and in other realms of existence: as a deva (angel) in a heavenly realm, or as a hungry ghost in a universe of terrible suffering. In these systems, human birth is considered precious, because it is as humans that we can best understand our predicament and work toward our liberation from the wheel of rebirth. In addition, human incarnations are rare. A Buddhist parable asks us to imagine that on one side of the world a blind turtle is set loose into the seven seas, while on the other side of the world, a wooden yoke is set to float freely on those same seas. The chance of the blind turtle surfacing with its head through

that yoke is the same slim chance we have of being reincarnated as humans.

A few members of our group have begun telling each
other what they want to be in their next lives. The Jester,
half serious, asks a Zen master, "Is it possible I could be
reincarnated in a place with no government?" The Zen
master smiles and replies, "With your karma you will probably be reborn as a vice-president." Meanwhile, a few
scientists who have been conferring come forward with a
statement, possibly hoping to reclaim the high ground from
the Asian sages. They contend that Eastern cosmologies
still talk as if time is an absolute that goes in one direction.
They conclude with the words of one of their own masters,
Albert Einstein, who wrote:

> People like us, who believe in physics, know that the
> distinction between past, present, and future is only a
> stubbornly persistent illusion.

Now wait a minute—if there is any such thing. Are all our
concepts of time, Eastern and Western alike, nothing but
fantasy? If no past, present, or future occurs, does that mean
we won't get old and die? If time in the conventional sense

doesn't exist, maybe we can all relax—there are no dead-lines to meet and we are instantly immortal. If there is no distinction between present and future, then maybe you, the reader, are reading this word at the same time it is being written. (If so, please think of a good sentence to follow this one.)

"Be here now!" The Zen master tries this again, but of course everybody misses it again except for one clown, who claims to have seized the moment and now offers to show it to anyone who wants to see. Meanwhile, most of our group members seem to have lost their bearings and appear dizzy or confused. The Taoist master explains that it is common to feel this way after looking deeply into the mysteries of space and time. After discovering that there is no center to the universe, no central standard time, no East, no West, no now, no then—there can be no way to get our bearings. We are bound to become dizzy, if not crazy and wise. For clarification, the Taoist sage recites from Chuang-tzu:

> There is no end to the weighing of things, no stop to time, no constancy to the division of lots, no fixed rule to beginning and end. Therefore great wisdom

observes both far and near, and for that reason recognizes small without considering it paltry, recognizes
large without considering it unwieldy, for it knows that
there is no end to the weighing of things. It has a clear
understanding of past and present, and for that reason
it spends a long time without finding it tedious, a short
time without fretting its shortness, for it knows that
time has no stop. It perceives the nature of fullness
and emptiness, and for that reason does not delight
if it acquires something nor worry if it loses it, for it
knows that there is no constancy to the division of lots.
It comprehends the Level Road, and for that reason it
does not rejoice in life nor look on death as a calamity,
for it knows that no fixed rule can be assigned to
beginning and end.

Could it be that we just can't know anything? Many in our
group are coming to this conclusion, if they weren't there
when we started. A biologist who is convinced of our
ignorance points out the irony in the fact that we have
labeled our species *"Homo sapiens sapiens,"* the human
who is very wise. Hearing this the Jester laughs and says,
"If we were really wise we would reclassify ourselves as
just humans, period. Then we wouldn't have so much to
live up to." The scientists, whose reputations and liveli-
hoods ride on this issue, hold their ground. Although we

may not understand the ultimate meaning of life, they assert, we are smart enough to learn the laws of nature and how the universe works. At this, the Taoist master smiles and says, "This belief continues in each new generation, in spite of a long, long history of mistakes."

What Do You Know?

Thou knowest no man can split the atom.

JOHN DALTON
British chemist and physicist responsible for the modern conception of atomic theory, 1803

Heavier-than-air flying machines are impossible.

LORD KEVLIN
British mathematician, physicist, and president of the British Royal Society, 1895

Looking back on the history of "knowledge," it becomes clear that it changes in every century and is different in each civilization. For example, people once knew that the world was flat and that the sun went around the earth. In fact, when we look back upon the history of knowledge, it seems something of a miracle that we have managed to survive our own ignorance. For example, Johann Hartmann, a seventeenth-century chemistry professor, was highly regarded in his time for his medical knowledge:

> For epilepsy in adults I recommend spirit of human brain or a powder, to be compounded only in May, June, and July, from the livers of live green frogs.

In spite of being "wrong," many ideas seem to have worked just fine for the people who knew them to be true. When the world was flat, nobody sailed out too far. When the sun rotated around earth, people still harvested their crops in the right season. Religious beliefs don't seem to have affected human destiny any more than scientific ones. When Zeus rather than Jehovah ruled the heavens, life was about the same: a mixture of joys and sorrows. The quality of life may not have much to do with knowledge or belief.

Perhaps the quest for any kind of certainty is doomed to failure. Taoists and Dadaists and good historians would bow to that. Now even scientists tell us that there is no fixed, objective knowledge—nothing independent of our subjective observations. In the end, there may be no "objective" truth, only "projective" truth. What we find always depends on what we think we need to know. The questions are always part of the answer.

Some crazy wisdom critics say our quest for knowledge is futile, although relatively harmless. Others contend that our desire to know has outlived its value as a survival mechanism and is getting in the way. The radical doubters and hard-line curmudgeons assert that our search has been a farce all along.

Adam and the Apple and the Atom and the Eve of Destruction

So when woman saw that the tree was good for food, and that it was a delight to the eyes, and that the tree was to be desired to make one wise, she took its fruit and ate; and she also gave some to her husband, and he ate.

GENESIS 3:6

The seeker is that which is being sought.

BUDDHIST SAYING

Curiosity killed the cat.

FOLK SAYING

The biblical story says that the pursuit of knowledge is what got us kicked out of the Garden of Eden. If Eve had not wanted to know what was going on, she wouldn't have eaten of the tree, and we might still be in Paradise today, wandering blissfully in naked innocence, passing time by enjoying the fruits that give no knowledge but sure taste good.

Our desire for certainty may have been born from a mixture of pride and fear, from our belief that we can know everything and our insecurity when we don't. In the twentieth century, scientific materialism led us to look for answers inside matter itself, as if by taking apart the world we could find a clue to the secrets of creation. The scientists split matter open; and they split it open again. And again. And when they finally got the atom they split that open, too. Inside the atom they did find the essence of all matter . . . and, lo and behold, it was energy! The tremendous, unspeakably pure power of the cosmos was hiding there inside of the smallest of things, holding matter together with an intricate and unimaginable force.

So great is the confusion of the world that comes from coveting knowledge!

CHUANG-TZU

There was knowledge inside the atom—just as there was knowledge inside the apple—and by discovering it, we may have angered the gods again. In our urgency to know, we have once again dared to steal the fire, the hidden sacred knowledge that could drive us even farther from the garden, and perhaps banish us from the planet forever.

The knowledge obtained from eating the apple in the Garden of Eden was the self-consciousness that divided up the universe and separated us from creation. However, the knowledge acquired from splitting the atom showed us that, at the most rudimentary level, all things are one. We are back where we started—before the Fall.

In splitting the atom, physicists found that matter and energy are interchangeable, which destroys the categories of both matter and energy. Now the two can't be separated; we are left with matter-energy, a reality held together by the dash. Space-time requires the same dash. Inside the dash, our logic and language cannot survive, but it may be the place where crazy wisdom lives. We know that all things require their opposite: Dark is necessary to light, death necessary to life, now needs then, yin is always getting ready to yang, and down is up and down simultaneously. To accept paradox is to accept what appears to be

> There are no facts, only interpretations.
>
> FRIEDRICH NIETZSCHE

the fundamental law of nature and rule of life. It might be that you can have your cake and eat it too. Or as physicist Neils Bohr puts it:

> A great truth is a truth whose opposite is also a great truth.

All truths are only half truths.
ALFRED NORTH WHITEHEAD

Most crazy wisdom masters understand that truth, like everything else, keeps changing. Our philosophies are continually overturned, and out scientific conclusions are reversed or shown to be only partially true. Descartes had a truth for his era, but now we blame him for the mind/body split. Newton was absolutely right about his universe, but not about other universes. Einstein's theories are being revised. Change may be the only constant in the universe. Truth is a verb.

Our Zen masters have stopped chanting and are teaching some of the clowns to how to meditate. The scientists are playing volleyball with the philosophers, and the Jester is sitting under a tree, staring into the distance. Coyote is nowhere to be found. Everybody in our crazy wisdom group seems tired. The Taoist sage explains what has happened: "The difficulty is that most of us are not content to just walk and look, we want to know everything. Another difficulty is that we not only don't know how not to know, we don't know how to know."

Think about It

The more the critical reason dominates, the more impoverished life becomes . . . .Overvalued reason has this in common with political absolutism: under its domination the individual is pauperized.

CARL JUNG

We are caught in a traffic jam of discursive thought.

CHÖGYAM TRUNGPA

Where do you think thinking has gotten us? Would we even be here if we didn't think, or to put it another way, would we have become extinct if we didn't think? Maybe we'd be "ex-thinkt." Descartes believed he wouldn't be here if he didn't think. He claimed, "I think, therefore I am." Perhaps he should have said, "I think, therefore, I think I am."

Of course we cannot, and do not wish to, dispense with the thinking process altogether, but we might learn how to use it better, and especially how to shut it off when appropriate. Much of our thinking is obsessive, a waste of energy, an extraneous feedback loop in the nervous system that is about as useful as the appendix. Do we really need the repetitious and gratuitous grinding of words and images, the chewing of mental cud? Furthermore, "critical reason" with which we constantly judge ourselves and the world, can be an alienating mode of thinking, tiresome and even painful.

Kurt Vonnegut takes a different stance from many when he claims that thinking is ineffective not because it is obsolete but because it is overdeveloped and possibly too advanced. In *Galapagos,* he looks back from the future to find:

> The mass of men was quietly desperate a million years ago because the infernal computers inside their skulls were incapable of restraint or idleness; were forever demanding more challenging problems . . . .

Vonnegut blames the problem on our "oversized brains," which do not fit our needs and circumstances. In *Wampeters, Foma, and Granfalloons,* he says, "The human brain is too high powered to have many practical uses in this particular universe." And again in *Galapagos,* "There was no end to the evil schemes that a thought machine that oversized couldn't imagine and execute."

Not only is thinking dangerous, it is highly overrated as a pastime. Many spiritual crazy wisdom masters suggest that you try "non-thinking" sometime. It feels good. It even feels wise. Some people think that non-thinking is "empty-headed." Quite true, the masters say, and don't knock it if you haven't tried it.

The jester Jonathan Swift didn't think much of thinking too much. In *Gulliver's Travels*, he describes strangely familiar creatures called Laputans:

> Their heads were reclined either to the right, or the left; one of their eyes turned inward, and the other directly up to the zenith. I observed here and there many who employed servants, with a blown bladder fastened like a flail to the end of a short stick, which they carried in their hands. In each bladder was a small quantity of dried peas or little pebbles. With these bladders they now and then hit the mouths and ears of those who stood near them, of which practice I could not then conceive the meaning; it seems, the minds of these people are so taken up with intense speculations, that they neither can speak, nor attend to the discourses of others, without being roused by some external sensation upon the organs of speech and hearing; for which reason, those persons who are able to afford it always keep a flapper in their family, as one of their domestics,

whose job it is, when two or more persons are in company, gently to strike with his bladder the mouth of him who is to speak, and the right ear of him to whom the speaker addresseth himself.

Through the characteristics of Laputans, Swift satirized the British of the early eighteenth century. Surely, today we are much more advanced in our ability to communicate.

Listen with your ear. Speak without forming words. Language turns against itself and is likely to cause injury.

RUMI

A Word by Any Other Name

The confusions which occupy us arise when language is like an engine idling, not when it is doing work.

LUDWIG WITTGENSTEIN

Some modern crazy wisdom critics have tracked down thinking disease to words themselves—what author Colin Wilson calls "the mind parasites"—the buzzing insects in the brain. (The Jester asks, "Is that what's bugging you?")

As the Lord said, Come ye therefore, let us go down, and there confound their tongue, that they may not understand one another's speech.

GENESIS

The fall from grace was a fall from the actual into the symbolic life. In fact, it may have been the word apple" that got stuck in Adam's throat. We seem to have become entranced by our ability to give names to creation, until we no longer understand that the word is not the thing. Wittgenstein illustrates the problem this way:

> How do I know that this color is red? It would be an answer to say: "I have learnt English."

Modern language philosophers and linguists investigate how we deceive ourselves with our sophisticated system of signs and symbols. They explain how our belief in the reality of words can create confusion, especially when the words are abstractions such as "love" or "democracy." Words that refer to vague emotional states or lofty political ideals can trigger responses that are completely inappropriate to a specific situation.

Oliver Sacks, who studied aphasics, realized that they could perceive, beneath language, a deeper truth communicated by a speaker's emotional and physical presence. Sacks noted, "One cannot lie to an aphasic. He cannot grasp your words, and so cannot be deceived by them . . . ."

Repeating a word again and again shows that in itself, without a use in a situation, it becomes meaningless.

LUDWIG WITTGENSTEIN

Holy fools claim that language abstracts us from the world, keeping us from direct, or intuitive, perception. Many spiritual seekers say language, with its subject/object relationships, tangles us in an illusion of separateness. The poet Rumi knew how words can hide reality:

> Do you know a word that doesn't refer to something?
> Have you picked and held a rose from R, O, S, E?
> You say the NAME. Now try to find the reality it names.
> Look at the moon in the sky, not the one in the lake.
> If you want to be free of your obsession with words
> and beautiful lettering, make one stroke down.
> There's no self, no characteristics,
> But a bright center where you have the knowledge
> The Prophets have, without books or interpreter.
>
> RUMI

A Buddhist aphorism cautions us against missing the moon because we are focused on the finger pointing at it. We might also take care not to miss the moon by assuming that today's moon is the same as yesterday's moon. The moon, too, is a process.

O, swear not by the moon, the wandering moon, that monthly changes in her circled orb.

WILLIAM SHAKESPEARE

Our language behaves as though reality were solid. On the simplest level, it positions a subject and an object, which we think of as "real," on opposite sides of a verb, which we think of as less than real. In Hopi language, the nouns are verbs; it is inherent in the language that everything is interacting or in process.

After all these words, our crazy wisdom characters are tired, and they begin to disperse. The Taoist master wanders off toward some misty mountains, while the Jester heads back to the city to look for work. The clowns have decided to join the circus. The Zen masters sit down to meditate, agreeing that the here and now is as good as any space-time. The scientists pack up their notes; they have decided to become socially responsible by studying global warming. A few philosophers want to go back to school to learn a trade. Meanwhile, Coyote is heard in the nearby bushes, taking part in some boisterous and energetic activity. He no doubt will be able to take care of himself. As the dust settles, we come upon a poem by Pablo Neruda, titled "Flies Enter a Closed Mouth," a perfect epitaph for our questions and wanderings:

> Why, with these red fires, are the rubies ready to
> burst into flame?
>
> Why is the heart of the topaz
> yellow with the honeycombs?

Language is a virus from outer space.

WILLIAM BURROUGHS

Why is it the rose's vagary
to change the color of its dreams?

Why did the emerald freeze
like a drowned submarine?

And why does the sky pale
in the starlight of June?

Where does the lizard buy
fresh paint for its tail?

Where does the salt get
that look of transparency?

Where did the coal sleep
before it awoke to its darkness?

And where, where does the tiger buy
the stripes of its mourning, its markings of gold?

When did the honeysuckle first
sense its own perfume?

When did the pine take account
of its fragrant conclusion?

When did the lemons learn
the same creed as the sun?

When did smoke learn how to fly?

When do roots talk with each other?

How do stars get their water?

Why is the scorpion venomous
and the elephant benign?

What are the tortoise's thoughts?

To which point do the shadows withdraw?

What is the song of rain's repetitions?

Where do birds go to die?

And why are leaves green?

What we know comes out to so little,
what we presume is so much,
what we learn, so laborious,
we can only ask questions and die.

Better save all our pride
for the city of the dead
and the day of the carrion:
there when the wind shifts
through the hollows of your skull
it will show you all manner of
enigmatical things, whispering truths in the
void where your ears used to be.

CHAPTER 9

Crazy Wisdom in the Here and Now

> What a fine comedy this world would be if one did not play a part in it.
>
> DENIS DIDEROT

The forces of change had a great romp through the twentieth century, overturning cherished beliefs and behavior and causing the planet itself to wobble in its orbit. In just one hundred years, the human species experienced an explosion of information and inventions, nothing less than revolution in our evolution. We created fantastic tools and toys and awesome new terrors that have transformed the landscapes of both our psyches and our continents—an ice age's worth of change in a single century. Within a minute of historical time we have redesigned the surface of our planet and redefined ourselves.

In a few brief decades, the prevailing ways of life were transformed from religious to secular, rural to urban, and industrial to technological. Airplanes, automobiles, radios, movies, televisions, and computers have scrambled cultures and customs worldwide. Every god and every flag in every corner of the planet has been challenged by the knowledge, if not the direct intervention, of the gods and flags of other regions.

Nothing remains as it was; no one is left untouched. Fortunately, in this time of tremendous upheaval, crazy wisdom is flourishing again and, speaking here through the jester Woody Allen, wants to let us know that:

> More than at any time in history mankind faces a crossroads. One path leads to despair and utter hopelessness, the other to total extinction. Let us pray that we have the wisdom to choose correctly.

We once had an Iron Age, and after a series of intervening ages we have come to the Age of Irony. The rapid changes of the last hundred years show us that there may be no such thing as progress, that for every step forward, we take at least one step backward. Maybe we don't even know forward from backward. In this time of great change, some have begun to see humanity as nothing more than a species of clowns, wobbling precariously on a shaky rung of the evolutionary ladder, wondering whether this support system will hold us, and whether the ladder is even leaning against the right wall.

In a standard cartoon image, a dignified man wearing top hat and tails walks jauntily along, self-assured and proud—and is about to slip on a banana peel. We can put

210 * The Essential Crazy Wisdom

our entire civilization under that top hat; we feel proud of our progress, certain of our direction, convinced of our understanding, and . . . whoops! "Hey, what about the ozone layer? Who knew about this greenhouse effect? Terrorism? Overpopulation? Nuclear waste? Why didn't somebody tell us this might happen?"

Around the year 1900, the collective human metabolism seemed to accelerate. Henry Ford built his first car in 1893 and the Wright brothers took their first flight in 1903. In 1899 the first magnetic sound recording was made, and in 1900 R.A. Fessenden transmitted human speech via radio waves. In 1900 no one could have predicted that, less than seventy years later, rockets would take humans to the moon and orbiting satellites would transmit both sound and moving pictures to all areas of the earth. The twentieth century exposed everyone to everyone else. Cultural diversity was devastated, and innocence became nearly impossible.

The first year of the twentieth century saw the detonation of an intellectual bomb—an explosive herald of the real bombs that would follow in mid-century. It happened in December 1900, when Max Planck formulated quantum theory and started a complete revolution in our

Matter first appeared 10^{-38} seconds or so after the Big Bang, and will all disappear maybe 10^{+40} seconds from now.

SHELDON GLASHOW

understanding of the way in which the universe works. Quantum mechanics eventually undermined the concept of linear cause and effect as well as the notions of scientific objectivity and absolute truth.

In 1900 we did not have the birth control pill or know how to create new species of life through genetic engineering. The exact nature of DNA was not discovered until 1953. In 1900 no antibiotics existed, and we did not even know how to make plastic. In 1900 nobody could have imagined today's Los Angeles, and not one person believed in rock and roll.

It was in the auspicious year 1900 that Sigmund Freud first published his *The Interpretation of Dreams*. No one's dreams have been the same since, and we have created some exceptional new nightmares. Back in 1900 it would have been inconceivable that during the next hundred years, humans would kill nearly one hundred million other human beings. But then, in 1900 only one and a half billion people inhabited the earth. Few people could have foreseen that (in spite of all the killing) the population would nearly double by the year 1950, and then double again by 1988! Some enterprising mathematician recently calculated that if the population continues to increase at the current rate, the weight of human bodies will exceed the weight of the planet itself by the year 3500.

While the human population has increased threefold in the past one hundred years, industrial production has increased by a factor of fifty. Four-fifths of all that industrial growth has come since 1950. Experts say the enormous amount of pollution caused by this burst of productivity is heating up the planet's atmosphere and threatening civilization. At the beginning of the century nobody thought that humans could create such an impact on the environment.

Only in the twentieth century did humans begin to threaten the evolution of life on earth. In the second half of the century, we discovered that the growth of civilization was destroying the habitat of other forms of life and threatening many species with extinction. In the early 1970s the United States started keeping the Endangered Species List, which reads like a *Who's Who* of the animal world. Experts estimate that *thousands* of species of plant, insect, and animal life become extinct every single year, primarily due to the destruction of the planet's ecosystems. Humans have not yet placed themselves on the Endangered Species List, since it is presumed that only having too *few* members of a species is what endangers it—not too many.

The Rise and Fall and Rise and Fall and Rise . . .

We learn from history that we learn nothing from history.

GEORGE BERNARD SHAW
The Revolutionist's Handbook

The twentieth century saw the rise and fall of several major empires as political boundaries were rearranged over and over again in record time. At the beginning of the century, Europe was the center of power in the world, with Britain, France, Holland, Portugal, and Spain claiming dominion over all the continents. By the First World War, the European empires had begun to disintegrate, and by the end of the century they were reduced to nothing but minor players in the geopolitical scheme. Only a few decades ago, the British were proud to say, "The sun never sets on the British Empire." Now all that is left are those few chilly little islands in the North Atlantic, and the sun hardly ever rises on the British Empire.

The European empires survived for several hundred years, but in the twentieth century the process of rise and

A nation never fails but by suicide.

RALPH WALDO EMERSON

No power on earth is stronger than the United States of America today, and none will be stronger than the United States of America in the future.

RICHARD M. NIXON

fall speeded up. Russia gained and lost a vast hegemony within several decades. In half a century Germany conquered half a continent and then lost it—twice.

The last half of the twentieth century was called the American century, as the United States took over many of the former European colonies with Coke and movies and dreams too rich ever to be fulfilled. Maybe America will be immune to the dictates of history and the fate of all previous empires and superpowers, but probably not.

If decline is America's fate, a holy fool might remind us that at the end of an empire there is really nothing to fear but fear itself. After all, Rome didn't *decline* in a day. During the collapse of the Roman Empire, many Romans probably didn't even notice it was happening, and a few centuries later the Romans started calling themselves Italians, and they seem to be doing fine today.

If decline is inevitable, accepting it without too much struggle would be the best approach. In the past, the world's great powers have stubbornly tried to hold on to their status and glory, bringing about prolonged wars and great suffering. If we could learn from the mistakes of the past, we might rewrite the blueprint for the decline. Perhaps the safest way to get down from the big imperial mountain is to walk, not fall.

Tribe follows tribe and nation follows nation
    like the waves of the sea.
It is the order of nations, and regret is useless.
Your time of decay may be distant but it will surely
    come,
for even the white man, whose God walked and
    talked with him
as friend with friend, cannot be exempt from the
    common destiny.
We may be brothers after all. We will see.

CHIEF SEALTH, 1855

And Then God Said, "Let There Be Crazy Wisdom . . ."

All great truths begin as blasphemies.

GEORGE BERNARD SHAW

The current age has been a rough time for God, as well as for God's creatures. In the 1960s the cover of an issue of *Time* magazine posed the question "Is God Dead?" The jester just laughed and said, "Of course, God is not dead. He's just having a midlife crisis."

In the last few centuries anthropologists and paleon-tologists have taken us around the world and into the past, exposing us to the gods and religions of all human cultures. What has been revealed is the relativity of all belief systems, but, this does not mean that our deities are not real. Every god and goddess helps to define and refine us, and therefore each is, in some sense, our creator. It is therefore more accurate to say that all our belief systems are true. Each religion gives us a place to rest our questions and our hearts. Whether we worship the sun or the "son," we always worship life itself; we worship ourselves.

Crazy wisdom invites you to step up and walk that thin line between blasphemy and a healthy, humorous skepticism, as we prepare to meet the gods.

> Irreverence is my only sacred cow.
>
> PAUL KRASSNER

The Hundred Thousand Names of G-d

The Ethiopians say that their gods are snub-nosed and black, the Thracians that theirs have light blue eyes and red hair.

XENOPHANES

According to the Judeo-Christian tradition, a male god named Jehovah created the heavens and the earth and everything else in just six days. The Bible says that God looked at His creation and "saw that it was good." Some crazy wisdom observers think this could be the first recorded use of irony.

For a different creation story, we go to a Bantu tribe in Africa, whose creator is named Bumba. In the beginning Bumba was alone except for darkness and water. Suddenly, he was smitten with agonizing stomach pains, and he vomited out the sun, and the moon, and all living creatures. That sounds plausible. The universe is the product of a stomachache.

If God lived on earth, people would break out all His windows.

HASIDIC SAYING

> That fear first created the gods is perhaps as true as anything so brief could be on so great a subject.
>
> GEORGE SANTAYANA

If you happen to be from the central region of southwest Africa, you would probably believe in the sky god Ndjambi, whose name can be spoken or written only on special occasions. Hopefully, this is one of them.

Meanwhile, goddesses are returning to the West. If we're lucky, they will arrive in time to save us from further subjugation at the hands of mythological machismo. Crazy wisdom followers may enjoy praying to the ancient female Chinese creator named Nu-gua, who formed the first human beings from yellow clay and also invented the flute. Nu-gua sounds like a sweet, playful deity. Wouldn't it be nicer to crawl into Nu-gua's lap for some Great Mother nurturing than to beg mercy or await judgment from a wrathful, jealous, though-shalt-have-no-other-gods-before-me male deity, whose name we shall not utter. As Joseph Campbell pointed out, "In our religion everything is prosaic, and very, very serious. You can't fool around with Yahweh."

In the modern world, strange as it may seem, many people still believe that theirs is the *only* god, and true believers still try to convert people to their brand of deity.

In the summer of 1985, when Pope John Paul visited the Republic of Central Africa, he appeared at a gathering

of tens of thousands of people. In full papal regalia, he celebrated communion, and when he was finished symbolically
eating the body and drinking the blood of his god, he gave a
speech, telling the Africans to stop practicing voodoo. As
Cole Porter once asked, "Who do that voodoo . . . ?"

Through the ages, one of the jester's favorite pastimes has
been lampooning gods and religions, and poking a little fun
at the seriousness of most beliefs and rituals. Ever since
humans first decided that a creature-like creator controlled
things and cared especially for us; ever since the first prayer
or sacrifice was sent up in the hope that something would
be sent back down, crazy wisdom jesters have been busy
laughing and spreading doubt.

The twentieth century has fostered some particularly
inspired irreverence. For instance, writer Philip Wylie
observed that "If Jesus came back today, he would be killed
again. But this time he would probably be electrocuted.
And from that moment on, people would start wearing little
electric chairs on chains around their necks." Lenny Bruce
attempted to deflate religious chauvinism and hypocrisy
with bits like this:

DEFINITION: God is the
shortest distance between
zero and infinity. In which
direction? one may ask. We
shall reply that His first name
is not Jack, but Plus-and-
Minus. And one should say +
God is the shortest distance
between 0 and infinity, in
either direction.

ALFRED JARRY

Pope John Paul would be
more popular if he called
himself Pope John Paul
George and Ringo.

PAUL KRASSNER

> Do not take the Buddha for the Ultimate. As I look at him, he is still like the hole in the privy.
>
> LIN-CHI (RINZAI)

You and I know what a Jew is—someone who killed our Lord, Jesus Christ. I don't know if we got much press on that in Illinois—we did this about two thousand years ago—two thousand years of Polack kids whacking the shit out of us coming home from school. There should be a statute of limitations for that crime. Why do you keep breaking our balls for this? Alright, I'll confess . . . my family did it. I found a note in my basement. It said:
> "We killed him.
> Signed,
> Morty."

As we saw earlier, Mark Twain had some bitterly humorous disagreements with Jehovah and Christianity. One passage, however, written in a more somber tone, stands out as one of the most complete indictments ever made against any god and that god's creation.

> The first time the Deity came down to earth, he brought life and death; when he came the second time, he brought hell.
>
> Life was not a valuable gift, but death was. Life was a fever-dream made up of joys embittered by sorrows, pleasure poisoned by pain; a dream that was a nightmare-confusion of spasmodic and fleeting delights, ecstasies, exultations, happinesses, interspersed with

long-drawn miseries, griefs, perils, horrors, disap-
pointments, defeats, humiliations, and despairs—
the heaviest curse devisable by divine ingenuity; but
death was sweet, death was gentle, death was kind;
death healed the bruised spirit and the broken heart,
and gave them rest and forgetfulness; death was man's
best friend; when man could endure life no longer,
death came and set him free.

In time, the Deity perceived that death was a mistake; a mistake in that it was insufficient; insufficient,
for the reason that while it was an admirable agent for
the inflicting of misery upon the survivor, it allowed
the dead person himself to escape from all further
persecution in the blessed refuge of the grave. This
was not satisfactory. A way must be contrived to
pursue the dead beyond the tomb.

The Deity pondered this matter during four thousand years unsuccessfully, but as soon as he came
down to earth and became a Christian his mind
cleared and he knew what to do. He invented hell,
and proclaimed it.

Now here is a curious thing. It is believed by everybody that while he was in heaven he was stern, hard,
resentful, jealous, and cruel; but that when he came
down to earth and assumed the name Jesus Christ, he
became the opposite of what he was before; that is to
say, he became sweet, and gentle, merciful, forgiving,
and all harshness disappeared from his nature and a

deep and yearning love for his poor human children took its place. Whereas it was as Jesus Christ that he devised hell and proclaimed it!

Twain's statements may seem outrageous, but if humans must be tested and judged, why shouldn't the gods be also? Unfortunately, few gods seem to have a sense of humor or much perspective on themselves. Despite being gods, they just can't seem to see the bigger picture. H. L. Mencken would like us to have a little sympathy for them. Looking back through history, he realized that just as every dog has its day, so does every god. In "Memorial Service," Mencken asks for a moment of silence for those gods who have passed away.

Where is the grave-yard of dead gods? What lingering mourner waters their mounds? There was a time when Jupiter was the king of the gods, and any man who doubted his puissance was *ipso facto* a barbarian and an ignoramus. But where in all the world is there a man who worships Jupiter to-day?

. . . Tezcatilpoca was almost as powerful: he consumed 25,000 virgins a year. Lead me to his tomb: I would weep, and hang a *couronne des perles*. But who knows where it is? Or where the grave of Quitzalcoatl

is? . . . Or Xiehtecutli? Or Centoetl, that sweet one? . . .
Or that of Dis, whom Caesar found to be the chief god
of the Celts? Or that of Tarves, the bull? Or that of
Moccos, the pig? . . . Or that of Mullo, the celestial
jack-ass? There was a time when the Irish revered all
these gods. . . . But to-day even the drunkest Irishman
laughs at them.

But they have company in oblivion: the hell of dead
gods is as crowded as the Presbyterian hell for babies.
Damona is there, and Esus, and Drunemeton, and
Silvana, and Dervones, and Adsalluta . . . and Mogons.
All mighty gods in their day, worshipped by millions,
full of demands and impositions, able to bind and
loose—all gods of the first class, not dilettanti. Men
labored for generations to build vast temples to them—
temples with stones as large as hay-wagons. The business of interpreting their whims occupied thousands
of priests, wizards . . . bishops, archbishops. To doubt
them was to die, usually at the stake. Armies took to
the field to defend them against infidels: villages were
burned, women and children were butchered, cattle
were driven off. Yet in the end they all withered and
died, and to-day there is none so poor to do them
reverence. . . .

Quickly, before lightning strikes us, we offer Jack Kerouac
the last word on god.

We must not judge God from
this world. It's just a study
that didn't come off. It's only
a master who could make
such a blunder.

VINCENT VAN GOGH

No,—what is God?
The impossible, the impeachable
Unimpeachable Prezi-dent
Of the Pepsodent Universe
But with no body & no brain
no business and no tie
no candle and no high
no wise and no smart guy
no nothing, no no-nothing,
no anything, no-word, yes-word,
everything, anything, God,
the guy that ain't a guy,
the things that can't be
and can
and is
and isn't

CHAPTER 10

Crazy Wisdom Does the Dance of Death

Of all mindfulness meditations,
That on death is supreme.

BUDDHA
The Parinirvana Sutra

Death, where is thy sting-a-ling-a-ling?

DOROTHY PARKER

As we come to the end of this crazy wisdom story, we come to death. Or else death finally comes to us. Everybody and everything dies. In some very real sense, crazy wisdom has been talking about death all along: the death of knowledge and truth, beliefs and philosophies; the death of art forms and political institutions, nations and empires; the death of gods and goddesses; even the death of planets and galaxies and universes. It is appropriate that we dance this last dance with crazy wisdom.

Each of us and all our offspring will disappear from earth. In a few billion years the sun will explode, and with that fiery event surely the earth will be destroyed. The Pyramids and the Eiffel Tower will be gone, and all copies of the Bible will have burned up. You may be thinking that by then, with luck, humans will have emigrated

How do I know that loving life is not a delusion? How do I know that in hating death I am not like a man who, having left home in his youth, has forgotten the way back?

CHUANG-TZU

from this planet into a more stable solar system. We must remember, however, that according to current astronomical understanding, the entire universe is either expanding into nothingness, or will eventually collapse back into a single particle. Whatever occurs, not even Shakespeare will survive.

What do we fear when we fear death? The loss of our selves? According to the holy fools there is no self; all we have to lose are our illusions. Death is simply a way of ending this painful separation, a way of dissolving back into the flow; a homecoming. Crazy wisdom says: "We have nothing to fear from death but nothing—and nothing is nothing to fear at all."

> I'm not afraid of dying. I just don't want to be there when it happens.
>
> WOODY ALLEN

> Death is just infinity closing in.
>
> JORGE LUIS BORGES

Perhaps the most tragic aspect of death is that we fear it so much. Recent research shows that people who are resuscitated medically, literally brought back from the dead, aren't too happy about the revival. Apparently they enjoyed being dead; they say it's very peaceful. As Mark Twain commented, "All say, 'How hard it is that we have to die'—a strange complaint to come from the mouths of people who have had to live."

Death is crazy wisdom's best friend and most important teacher. When we get to know our own death and ask it to move in with us, all things assume their proper perspective. Rumi puts it this way:

> Why fear grief
> when Death walks so close beside?
> Don't fear the General
> If you are good friends with the Prince.

The holy fools of Asia have developed many ways to become friendly with death. Most meditation practices can be understood as a rehearsal for death, an exercise in letting go of each moment. Some Hindu and Buddhist yogis meditate at graveyards and cremation grounds to become intimate with the process of decay and transformation. Tibetan monks blow ceremonial horns made from human femurs and eat out of bowls carved from human skulls. In these actions, they partake of life in the face of death, thereby becoming more intimate with both.

From the perspective of life, which is the only perspective available to us, death is nothing to fear. Crazy

> The happiness of the drop is to die in the river.
> AL-GHAZALI

wisdom tries to explain it this way: If life is a joke, death is the punch line. If life is a tragedy, death means the show is over and we can leave for home. If we have many lives, as believed in the East, then we must also have many deaths, so we might as well get good at dying. Also, some sages say that only by learning how to die do we finally learn how to live. What an idea! Two lessons in one!

But wait. As usual, there's a catch. Those same sages will also tell us that once we learn how to live, we finally get off the wheel of rebirth. In other words, just when we get it right, the game is over.

In this excerpt from the book *Journey to Ixtlan*, the sorcerer Don Juan tells Carlos Castaneda to keep death over his left shoulder.

> "The thing to do when you're impatient," he proceeded, "is to turn to your left and ask advice from your death. An immense amount of pettiness is dropped if your death makes a gesture to you, or if you catch a glimpse of it, or if you just have the feeling that your companion is there watching you."

Every form is subject to transformation. That is the law of nature. And so each of us goes from womb to world to

The birth of man is the birth of his sorrow. The longer he lives, the more stupid he becomes, because his anxiety to avoid unavoidable death becomes more and more acute. What bitterness! He lives for what is always out of reach! His thirst for survival in the future makes him incapable of living in the present.
CHUANG-TZU

All conditioned things are impermanent. Work out your own salvation with diligence.
THE BUDDHA'S LAST WORDS

tomb to worms, just as our species travels from waves to caves to graves and, some would say, back to the start again. Every ending is also a beginning, and death surely leads somewhere. We do know that without death for comparison, there would be no such thing as life. So here's to death! Thanks a lot.

Death Poems and Epitaphs

A crazy wisdom tradition among poets, artists, and Zen monks in Japan is to write a death poem as one approaches the final moments. It is considered cheating to write the death poem before you are quite sure that death is imminent, since the poem is a final test of your attitude toward death, a testament to your level of spiritual attainment. On their deathbeds, the masters are fearless, in full control of their artistic powers, and ready with wry perceptions of crazy wisdom.

BENJAMIN FRANKLIN'S
EPITAPH:
The Body of B. Franklin,
    Printer
Like the Cover of an Old Book
Its Contents Torn Out And
Stripped of its Lettering and
    Gilding,
Lies Here
Food for Worms
But the Work Shall not be
    Lost,
For it Will as He Believed
Appear Once More
In a New and more Elegant
    Edition
Revised and Corrected
By the Author

From one basin
to another—
stuff and nonsense.

ISSA

Bury me when I die
beneath a wine barrel
in a tavern.
With luck
The cask will leak.

MORIYA SEN' AN

This must be
my birthday there
in paradise.

JOSEKI

Till now I thought
that death befell
the untalented alone.
If those with talent,
    too, must die
surely they make
a better manure?

KYORIKU

My old body:
a drop of dew grown
heavy at the leaf tip.

KIBA

Though I should live
To be a hundred,
The same world,
    the same cherry-blossoms;
The moon is round,
The snow is white.

TAIYA TEIRYU

A few days before his death, Zen teacher Kozan Ichikyo called his pupils together and ordered them to bury him without ceremony, forbidding them to hold services in his memory. He wrote the following poem on the morning of his death, laid down his brush, and died sitting upright.

Empty-handed I entered the world
Barefoot I leave it.
My coming, my going—
Two simple happenings
That got entangled.

While living
Be a dead man
Be thoroughly dead—
And Behave as you like,
And all's well.

BUNAN, ZEN MASTER

WILLIAM BUTLER YEATS'S
EPITAPH:
Cast a cold eye
On life, on death.
Horseman, pass by!

It is customary and auspicious for Zen monks to die while sitting in meditation. Chinese Zen Master Chihhsien asked his disciples, "Who dies sitting?" They answered, "A monk." Then he asked, "Who dies standing?" His disciples answered, "Enlightened monks." Chihhsien then took seven steps and died standing up.

In *Oriental Humor*, R. H. Blyth tells of an even more impressive exit: Zen monk Teng Yinfeng asked his followers whether anyone had ever died upside down. When they told him it had never been seen or heard of, Teng stood on his head and died. A great closing act for a great fool.

CHAPTER 11

The End Is Also the Middle

And I am not a demigod,
I cannot make it cohere.

EZRA POUND
Canto XVI

It may not be wise to draw any conclusions from what's been said in this book, but it would be crazy not to try. In any case there are several good quotations left that might go nicely into a summary. So let us begin to conclude. As Groucho Marx might say, "Hello . . . I must be going."

We have heard many different voices singing variations on the crazy wisdom themes, and the most common refrain is that we can't be sure about much of anything. As soon as we become too certain of our understanding, the trickster arises to switch the shape of things or reveal another layer of reality. According to crazy wisdom, truth's name is transformation.

Crazy wisdom points out that everything we know, everything we believe, and everything we are is destined to evolve or dissolve into something else. Life transforms from microbe to monkey to man. Man raises a flag, only to have it lowered and another one unfurled in its place. Gods come and go, and new scientific and artistic movements arise to

The torch of doubt and chaos, this is what the sage steers by.

CHUANG-TZU

show us truth and beauty from different angles. Meanwhile, the universe continues on toward an unknown destiny about which we can only speculate.

Throughout this book, we have heard holy fools and mad modern scientists talking about the unity of all things. They tell us that, while distinctions and separations may be of some practical use, in essence they are illusions. According to crazy wisdom, reality rests easier in the center of the paradox, in the slashes and dashes that join all things together: matter-energy, space-time, particle-wave, either/or, this/that, us/them.

Life itself is paradox—both meaningful and meaningless, important and insignificant, a joke and a yoke. These mutually exclusive qualities exist simultaneously, just as wave and particle do in the subatomic world. For all practical purposes, life is many things at once. Poet Robert Frost captures this understanding with a line he wanted engraved on his tombstone:

I had a lover's quarrel with the world.

If there is any central message in *The Essential Crazy Wisdom,* it is simply that we need not take ourselves quite

We are here and it is now. Further than that all human knowledge is moonshine.
H. L. MENCKEN

> He who knows he is a fool is not the biggest fool; he who knows he is confused is not in the worst confusion.
>
> CHUANG-TZU

> The most fundamental of divisions is that between the intellect, which can only do its work by saying continually 'thou fool,' and the religious genius which makes it all equal.
>
> WILLIAM BUTLER YEATS

so seriously. If all things are constantly transforming and will eventually die, then perhaps the best way to live is not by holding on, but by *letting go with all our might*—letting go of our impossible craving for certainty or significance; letting go of our demands on the universe for perfect happiness and everlasting life. Our only option may be to learn what Alan Watts called "the wisdom of insecurity" and to discover that which Camus sought—a way to be comfortable with unfamiliarity. We are then free to leap with Chuang-tzu into "the boundless" and make it our home. Accepting uncertainty as our philosophy might allow us to honor each other's stories more, delighting in all the bizarre and wondrous interpretations of the mystery. We might also show more tolerance for those who appear to be fools and for those who speak truths we don't wish to hear.

The very existence of crazy wisdom implies that another kind of intelligence might arise once we accept our ignorance and our limitations. A better balance of doing and being may then be possible. As Jean-Paul Sartre said, "Everything has been figured out, except how to live."

Given the brevity of our existence and the fact that we don't know what it means or what we are supposed to be doing here, perhaps our only recourse is to learn how to be in the moment with what is before us. This sentiment has been expressed in different ways by many sages, most often in the simplest of terms:

> Don't worry, be happy.
> MEHER BABA

> What, me worry?
> ALFRED E. NEUMAN

These few words may sound too simplistic to those for whom reality implies difficulty and complexity. Nonetheless, many holy fools have emphasized simplicity of thought and living as the path to harmony and, therefore, the ultimate human virtue. Some crazy wisdom masters tell us that slowing down may actually be progress, and that just sitting still may be one of the most useful of all activities. To elaborate on this sentiment, we leave with the statement of a poet, Pablo Neruda, offering us some final words of crazy wisdom.

> Students achieving oneness will move ahead to twoness.
> WOODY ALLEN

KEEPING QUIET
Now we will count to twelve
and we will all keep still
for once on the face of the
earth,
let's not speak in any language;
let's stop for a second,
and not move our arms so much.

It would be an exotic moment
without rush, without engines;
we would all be together
in a sudden strangeness.

Fishermen in the cold sea
would not harm whales
and the man gathering salt
would not look at his hurt hands.

Those who prepare green wars,
wars with gas, wars with fire,
victories with no survivors,
would put on clean clothes
and walk about with their brothers
in the shade, doing nothing.

What I want should not be confused
with total inactivity.
life is what it is about; . . .

If we were not so single-minded
about keeping our lives moving,
and for once could do nothing,
perhaps a huge silence
might interrupt this sadness
of never understanding ourselves
and of threatening ourselves with
death.

Perhaps the earth can teach us
as when everything seems to be dead in winter
and later proves to be alive.

Now I'll count up to twelve
and you keep quiet and I will go.

About the Author

WES NISKER is a journalist, author, and Buddhist meditation teacher. For the past twenty years he has been leading retreats and workshops worldwide in philosophy, humor, and Buddhist insight meditation. Mr. Nisker is the founder and coeditor of the international Buddhist journal *Inquiring Mind,* and the author of two best-selling books, including the original *Crazy Wisdom* and *Buddha's Nature: A Guide to Finding Your Place in the Cosmos.* Mr. Nisker is also a radio journalist, well known in the San Francisco Bay Area as "Scoop." His radio work has won many honors, including the Billboard magazine and Columbia School of Journalism awards for excellence in radio programming. Mr. Nisker is an affiliate of the Spirit Rock Meditation Center in Woodacre, California.